SpringerBriefs in Criminology

More information about this series at http://www.springer.com/series/10159

Clare Farmer

Discretionary Police Powers to Punish

A Case Study of Victoria's Banning Notice Provisions

Springer

Clare Farmer
School of Humanities and Social Sciences
Deakin University
Waurn Ponds, Geelong, VIC
Australia

ISSN 2192-8533 ISSN 2192-8541 (electronic)
SpringerBriefs in Criminology
ISBN 978-981-10-8868-1 ISBN 978-981-10-8869-8 (eBook)
https://doi.org/10.1007/978-981-10-8869-8

Library of Congress Control Number: 2018934950

Printed on acid-free paper

This Springer imprint is published by the registered company Springer Nature Singapore Pte Ltd.
part of Springer Nature
The registered company address is: 152 Beach Road, #21-01/04 Gateway East, Singapore 189721, Singapore

Preface

Alcohol-related disorder in and around licensed premises continues to generate significant public interest and is an area of ongoing legislative and policing developments. Banning notices sit within a range of provisions enacted to address behavioural problems within urban entertainment precincts. Banning notices embody a move towards police-imposed summary justice, which is circumventing the criminal law, operating without effective oversight, and reconfiguring the notion of balance within the criminal justice system.

Victoria was the first Australian jurisdiction to introduce alcohol-related police-imposed on-the-spot banning powers, in December 2007. This book provides an analysis of the justifications which ensured their passage through the Victorian Parliament, identifies key deficiencies with respect to the scrutiny of the use of banning powers, and sets out notable issues regarding individual rights, the circumvention of due process, and the effect on criminal justice processes. The specific findings sit within and support a body of international research addressing punishments which are discretionary, prohibitive or pre-emptive, and which serve to increasingly dilute individual rights.

This book presents an applied Australian example of mixed methodological research in the field of criminology, which will support the teaching and understanding of research which utilises multiple research methods.

The author offers sincere thanks to those who reviewed the proposal and draft versions of this book, for their time, feedback, and helpful recommendations, and to the editorial and production team at Springer.

To Matt, Tom, Ethan, Baci, and Sami—thank you for your enduring support and capacity to distract.

Waurn Ponds, Geelong, Australia　　Clare Farmer

Contents

Chapter 1
Introduction

Abstract This book examines Victoria's banning notice provisions and applies a mixed methodological approach to explore two core themes. The first analyses underlying assumptions and justifications used to secure the passage of the banning notice provisions through the Victorian Parliament in 2007. The second theme considers the ongoing failure to review the use of the banning legislation or to test the assumptions and justifications upon which it was predicated. This introductory chapter sets out the key themes and how they are examined.

Over the past decade alcohol-related violence and disorder in and around licensed premises has been an area of considerable legislative, licensing and operational policing development. Across international[1] and Australian jurisdictions, police officers have been afforded a range of powers to tackle problems associated with excessive alcohol consumption. New offences and infringement penalties have been introduced along with move-on provisions and powers of exclusion. Many of the new provisions empower police officers to make subjective, on-the-spot decisions to impose an immediate punishment, such as to move-on or be excluded from a given area. These discretionary powers to punish can undermine expectations of procedural justice and limit the individual rights of those receiving the punishments.

In the state of Victoria, in Australia, the burgeoning night-time economy (NTE) reflected significant growth in the alcohol industry following the 1986 Nieuwenhuysen Report. Liquor licence reforms, taxation changes and deregulation facilitated a proliferation of licensed venues, the growth of urban entertainment precincts across the State,[2] and the escalation of alcohol-related problems. Victoria's Alcohol Action Plan: 2008–13 (Department of Justice 2008) presented a suite of initiatives targeting a reduction in the impact of alcohol-fuelled violence and anti-social behaviour. A key element of the plan was the introduction of police-imposed banning notices.

[1]Examples include England and Wales, the USA, and Canada.

[2]Between 1995–2005 the number of licensed premises in Victoria rose from 2000 to 24,000 (Alcohol Policy Coalition 2011, p. 6).

C. Farmer, *Discretionary Police Powers to Punish*, SpringerBriefs in Criminology,
https://doi.org/10.1007/978-981-10-8869-8_1

Banning has been available as an option within Victoria's court-imposed penalties for over a decade, and for longer by venue licensees under common law and trespass provisions.[3] The first police-imposed 24 hour banning notice powers were enacted under the *Liquor Control Reform Amendment Act 2007* (Vic) ('*LCRA Act 2007*'). The *Justice Legislation Amendment (Victims of Crime Assistance & Other Matters) Act 2010* (Vic) ('*JLA Act 2010*') extended their permissible length of a ban to 72 hour. Banning notices apply in designated areas,[4] and may be imposed for a range of specified offences or pre-emptively to prevent a further offence or a perceived future problematic behaviour. A decision to issue a banning notice is made subjectively by a police officer. Recipients must leave the designated area and not return for a fixed period. The banning notice applies immediately, must be accepted, requires no evidence to be recorded, and a decision to ban is not subject to independent or judicial appeal.

Victoria's banning notice provisions provide a clear challenge to the conception of balance within the criminal justice system. The discretionary and potentially pre-emptive powers afforded to police officers, and the consequential effect of banning notices upon core individual rights and judicial safeguards, undermine the principle of the separation of powers and the expectation of due process in the administration of justice.

There has been only limited analysis of Victoria's banning notices (Palmer and Warren 2014; Farmer 2014, 2016, 2017a, b; Curtis et al. 2018)[5] and the exclusionary principles they embody.[6] To mark a decade since the introduction of police-imposed banning in Victoria, this book reflects upon Victoria's banning notice provisions, and applies a mixed methodological approach to examine two core themes. The first considers the underlying assumptions and justifications that secured the passage of the banning provisions through the Victorian Parliament. The second theme explores the ongoing failure to review the use of the banning legislation, or to test the presump-

[3]For example, under s9(1)(d) of the *Summary Offences Act 1966* (Vic).

[4]A designated area may be declared by the Victorian Commission for Gambling and Liquor Regulation (VCGLR) in response to recorded incidents of alcohol-related disorder.

[5]Palmer and Warren (2014) set Victoria's banning provisions within broader exclusionary principles. Farmer (2014) responds to a question posed during the 2007 parliamentary debates of the banning notice bill, and considers 'is a 24 hour ban such a bad thing?' Farmer (2016) examines the passage of the banning notice bills through the Victorian Parliament and highlights notable procedural and individual vulnerabilities inherent in the provisions and their implementation. Farmer (2017a) explores the application of the compliance requirements of Victoria's *Charter of Human Rights and Responsibilities Act 2006* to the banning provisions, and sets out key disparities between human rights policy and parliamentary practice. Farmer (2017b) considers Victoria's banning notice powers in the context of collective 'pre-victimisation' and the dilution of individual rights. Key findings from these papers are acknowledged, extended and synthesized in this book. Curtis et al. (2018) provides an introductory consideration of the potential deterrent effect of banning provisions in Victoria.

[6]A significant body of literature has examined exclusion and the policing of space across a variety of criminal justice contexts. Examples include, MacDonald (1997), Young (1999), Garland (2001), Travis (2002), Hermer and Mosher (2002), Gaetz (2004), Belina (2007), Beckett and Herbert (2010a, b), Aas (2011), Ewald (2011). However, the broader exclusionary tradition is not a focus of this book.

tions upon which it was predicated. Broader consequences of discretionary police powers to punish are also considered; including their effect upon individual rights, the expectations of balance within criminal processes, and the steady and largely unchecked proliferation of similar banning powers across Australian jurisdictions (Farmer et al. 2017). The specific findings are set within a broader discussion of concerns regarding pre-emptive and preventive justice in comparative international jurisdictions.[7]

Chapter 2 provides an overview of discretionary summary justice, the expanding scope of police powers, blurring of criminal and civil boundaries, and the increasing use of pre-emptive controls. The interplay between human rights, the drive to ensure security, risk mitigation and community protection, and the contentious notion of 'balance' are also examined. Key influences for and consequences of the 're-balancing' agenda are outlined, along with consideration of the centrality of human rights in the development of legislation.

Chapter 3 summarises Victoria's banning notice provisions, and outlines the research design upon which the findings and analysis within this chapter are based. The key arguments and rhetoric that supported the passage of the banning legislation through the Victorian Parliament are explored, along with consideration of the compliance requirements of Victoria's Charter of Human Rights and Responsibilities Act 2006. In the context of concern about a lack of understanding of the effect of police-imposed summary justice (Crawford 2009), and disquiet about the erosion of due process rights (Zedner 2005; Ashworth 2006; Ashworth and Zedner 2008), the final part of the chapter examines the ongoing public scrutiny of the discretionary police power to ban. Published data from Victoria Police, media analysis, and interviews with Victorian Magistrates inform consideration of the extent to which police officers have been held accountable for their discretionary powers to punish.

Chapter 4 sets the key research findings within a broader context of concern regarding the consequences of discretionary police powers to punish. Victoria's police-imposed on-the-spot banning provisions were introduced to address issues of alcohol-related disorder in the NTE. They reflect a trend, evident across many Western jurisdictions, that seeks to 're-balance' criminal justice processes under the auspices of national security and public safety, by prioritising the collective needs of community protection and legitimising the dilution of individual due process rights. However, banning notices undermine core due process protections and subsume the rights of individuals to a perceived need for community protection. That the effect of banning notices upon the individual rights of recipients were either not recognised or were disregarded during the process of enactment has significant implications for the administration of justice and conceptions of balance. These consequences are exacerbated by a failure to monitor the way in which banning notices, and the discretionary police powers that they embody, are used. Rather than re-balancing criminal justice processes, Victoria's banning notices remove long standing due process protections and individual rights, for a need that is unsubstantiated and with an effect that is unknown.

[7]For example, the UK, USA and Canada.

References

Aas, K. F. (2011). 'Crimmigrant' bodies and bona fide travellers: Surveillance, citizenship and global governance. *Theoretical Criminology, 15*(3), 331–346.

Alcohol Policy Coalition. (2011). *Submission to the whole of government Victorian alcohol and drug strategy*. Melbourne: Alcohol Policy Coalition.

Ashworth, A. (2006). Four threats to the presumption of innocence. *The International Journal of Evidence and Proof, 10,* 241–279.

Ashworth, A., & Zedner, L. (2008). Defending the criminal law: Reflections on the changing character of crime, procedure and sanctions. *Criminal Law and Philosophy, 2,* 21–51.

Beckett, K., & Herbert, S. (2010a). *Banished. The new social control in Urban America*. New York: Oxford University Press.

Beckett, K., & Herbert, S. (2010b). Penal boundaries; banishment and the expansion of punishment. *Law & Social Inquiry, 35*(1), 1–38.

Belina, B. (2007). From disciplining to dislocation: Area bans in recent urban policing in Germany. *European Urban and Regional Studies, 14*(4), 321–336.

Crawford, A. (2009). Governing through anti-social behaviour: Regulatory challenges to criminal justice. *British Journal of Criminology, 49*(6), 810–831.

Curtis, A., Taylor, N., Guadagno, B., Farmer, C., & Miller, P. (2018). Community awareness of patron banning in Australia: A brief report. *Journal of Police and Criminal Psychology* [in press].

Department of Justice, Victoria. (2008). *Victoria's alcohol action plan: 2008–2013*. Melbourne: State Government of Victoria.

Ewald, A. C. (2011). Collateral consequences and the perils of categorial ambiguity. In A. Sarat, L. Douglas, & M. M. Umphrey (Eds.), *Law as punishment, law as regulation* (pp. 77–123). Stanford, California: Stanford University Press.

Farmer, C. (2014). Is a 24-hour ban such a bad thing? *Australian Journal of Human Rights, 20*(2), 39–62.

Farmer, C. (2016). Victoria's banning notice provisions: parliamentary, procedural and individual vulnerabilities. *Journal of Criminological Research, Policy & Practice, 2*(3), 173–184.

Farmer, C. (2017a). The disparity between human rights policy and parliamentary practice in Australia: A Victorian case study. *The International Journal of Human Rights, 27*(2), 167–188.

Farmer, C. (2017b). Upholding whose right? Discretionary police powers to punish, collective 'pre-victimisation' and the dilution of individual rights. *Australian & New Zealand Journal of Criminology, 50*(4), 493–509.

Farmer, C., Curtis, A., & Miller, P. (2017). The steady proliferation of Australia's discretionary police-imposed banning powers: An unsubstantiated cycle of assertion and presumption. *Criminology & Criminal Justice* [published online 27/9/17].

Gaetz, S. (2004). Safe streets for whom? Homeless youth, social exclusion and criminal victimisation. *Canadian Journal of Criminology and Criminal Justice, 46*(4), 423–456.

Garland, D. (2001). *The culture of control: Crime and social order in contemporary society*. Oxford: Oxford University Press.

Hermer, J., & Mosher, J. (2002). *Disorderly people: Law and the politics of exclusion in Ontario*. Halifax, Nova Scotia: Fernwood Publishing.

MacDonald, R. (1997). *Youth, the 'Underclass' and social exclusion*. London: Routledge.

Nieuwenhuysen, J. (1986). *Review of the liquor control reform act 1968*. Melbourne: Victorian Government.

Palmer, D., & Warren, I. (2014). The pursuit of exclusion through zonal banning. *Australian & New Zealand Journal of Criminology, 47*(3), 429–446.

Travis, J. (2002). Invisible punishment: An instrument of social exclusion. In M. Mauer & M. Chesney-Lind (Eds.), *Invisible punishment: The collateral consequences of mass imprisonment* (pp. 15–36). New York: The New Press.

Young, J. (1999). *The exclusive society: Social exclusion, crime and difference in late modernity*. London: Sage Publications.

Zedner, L. (2005). Securing liberty in the face of terror; Reflections from criminal justice. *Journal of law and society, 32*(4), 507–533.

Chapter 2
Discretionary Summary Justice

Abstract Anti-social behaviour and alcohol-related violence in and around licensed premises have generated significant public interest, and become an area of notable legislative and operational policing developments. A common theme, explored in this chapter, is the discretionary and often prohibitive nature of police powers which are enacted under the auspices of preventative justice. Key developments and debate from Australian and comparative jurisdictions overseas are examined in the first part of this chapter. Victoria's banning notices sit within a range of provisions enacted in response to problems of disorderly behaviour, in the night-time economy and a range of other contexts. The legal principles on which banning notices are based and the way in which they are implemented challenge traditional expectations regarding the separation of powers and individual due process rights in the administration of justice. Banning notices are one example of a move towards police-imposed summary justice, which circumvents the criminal law, removes effective oversight, and reconfigures the notion of balance in the criminal justice system. The second part of this chapter discusses key issues that this reconfiguration may embody, and considers why this matters.

2.1 The Criminal Process in Victoria

The criminal process encompasses two core principles of the Australian constitutional system—the rule of law and the separation of powers. The rule of law embodies the expectation that everyone, citizens and government, are subject to the laws that are enacted by parliament (Walker 1988). It is predicated upon the separation of the powers of government into three distinct entities: the executive, the legislature and the judiciary. The right to determine specific criminal laws in Australia is largely devolved to the states and territories (*Commonwealth of Australia Constitution Act 1900,* s118). The *Constitution Act 1975* sets out the Victorian Parliament's right to determine the state's criminal laws.

The rights of those affected by the criminal process are fundamental to the expression of balance in the criminal justice system. While determinations made by the High Court of Australia have served to read certain human rights guarantees into the Consti-

C. Farmer, *Discretionary Police Powers to Punish*, SpringerBriefs in Criminology,
https://doi.org/10.1007/978-981-10-8869-8_2

tution (French 2009), Australia has no formal Bill of Rights and none are specified in Victoria's *Constitution Act 1975*. Core individual rights and civil liberties are derived from post Magna Carta legal instruments and common law tradition emanating from England and Wales (Castles 1982; Keon-Cohen 1991; Lord Irvine of Lairg 2002).[1] Fundamental rights such as freedom of movement, natural justice and access to the courts have been framed as a "common law bill of rights" (Spigelman 2008, p. 29). Due process extends the principle of natural justice to protect the rights of individuals in their treatment by the agencies of the criminal justice system, and to ensure procedural fairness in the administration of justice (Galligan 1996; Rares 2013). Specific due process rights include the presumption of innocence, the right to legal representation, and the right to a fair trial (Blake and Ashworth 1996; Wheeler 1997, 2004; Ashworth 2006a; Keyzer 2008; Bateman 2009; Findley 2009). In the absence of a federal Bill of Rights such due process rights have been enshrined through long-standing use and expectation (Castles 1982; French 2009). More recently individual rights have been increasingly formalised through international conventions to which Australia is a signatory,[2] via the Commonwealth Parliamentary Joint Committee on Human Rights (established by the *Human Rights (Parliamentary Scrutiny) Act 2011*), and in provisions such as the Australian Capital Territory's *Human Rights Act 2004*, and Victoria's *Charter of Human Rights and Responsibilities 2006* ('the Charter/*Charter Act*').

The *Charter Act* provides a commitment that the civil, political, cultural and due process rights afforded to all citizens of Victoria will be upheld, and that these rights will be protected in legislative decision-making. The Charter articulates the specific rights regarded as "essential in a democratic and inclusive society that respects the rule of law, human dignity, equality and freedom" (*Charter Act* 2006, preamble). This includes fundamental due process protections in relation to criminal proceedings, such as the presumption of innocence, a fair hearing, and the right to appeal a conviction and sentence. However, the *Charter Act* acknowledges that individual rights are not inviolable, and may be subject to reasonable limitations. A Ministerial Statement of Compatibility must accompany each new Bill to confirm adherence to the Charter (*Charter Act 2006*, s28). Any measures in a Bill that do not comply with one or more Charter rights must be justified, and the need must be empirically evidenced in the Statement of Compatibility (*Charter Act 2006*, s7(2)). Section 31 of the *Charter Act* includes an override mechanism, whereby the Victorian Parliament may

---

[1] The Magna Carta makes clear the expectation of 'due process' in the administration of justice, albeit for freemen: "No free man shall be seized or imprisoned, or stripped of his rights or possessions, or outlawed or exiled, or deprived of his standing in any way, nor will we proceed with force against him, or send others to do so, except by the lawful judgement of his equals or by the law of the land" (full text translation: British Library n.d.). In *Momcilovic v The Queen & Ors* (2011) HCA 34, French CJ observed that most rights derive from the common law.

[2] Australia played a key role in drafting the United Nations' *Universal Declaration of Human Rights 1948*, and is bound, with stated reservations, by the *International Convention on Civil & Political Rights 1966* (ICCPR) (AHRC n.d). Australia is also a signatory to the *International Covenant on Economic, Social & Cultural Rights 1966* (ICESCR) and other human rights instruments, including the *Convention on the Rights of the Child 1989*. Compliance is monitored by the Commonwealth Parliamentary Joint Committee on Human Rights (Parliament of Australia n.d.).

expressly declare, in "exceptional circumstances" (s31(4)), that an Act "has effect despite being incompatible with one or more of the human rights or despite anything else set out in this Charter" (s31(1)).[3] Despite the passage of the *Charter Act*, the primacy of parliamentary law making power in Victoria provides the foundation for the state to erode core rights and due process safeguards (Rares 2013).

2.1.1 The Steady Dilution of Individual Rights

The underlying criminal justice process in Victoria extends the principle of the separation of executive, legislative and judicial powers. Clear parameters should ensure consistency, transparency, accountability, and effective preservation of individual rights and due process protections. In recent decades, perceived public anxieties about high profile issues, such as national security, crime and anti-social behaviour, have coincided with a range of legislative responses and changes to the criminal process. Governments in a number of English-speaking jurisdictions, such as the UK, USA and Australia, have used political expedience and media-driven hysteria to justify a steady dilution of individual rights. Recurring and specific changes have been documented across a body of literature; key themes include the increasing use of discretionary police decision-making and summary justice, the blurring of boundaries between civil and criminal methods of determining liability, the use of pre-emptive police powers to punish, and the criminalisation of an expanding range of anti-social behaviours.[4] Justified by rhetoric that a higher purpose is being served by addressing a pressing socio-political issue, the effect upon the separation of powers and individual due process rights have been largely overlooked during the legislative process, or subsumed by claims of a greater good, political expedience or parliamentary indifference.

Valverde suggested that "the effect of the game is that the crucial question of how governance is done ends up being decided without explicit discussion" (2009, p. 145). Failure to adequately consider the consequences of legislative and operational responses to perceived issues of security or disorder are fundamental concerns for the protection of individual rights (Farmer 2017a, b). The significance of changes to the criminal process is embodied in Crawford's (2009) depiction of the 'net-widening' effect of policing by discretionary summary justice.[5] Crawford examines the increase in the range of behaviours that may lead to a police-imposed penalty, and the resulting

---

[3]An override declaration lasts for up to five years and can be extended.

[4]See, for example, Ashworth (2004, 2006a), Zedner (2005, 2007a, b, c, 2014), Von Hirsch and Simester (2006), Ashworth and Zedner (2008, 2015), Squires (2008), Beckett and Herbert (2008, 2009, 2010a, b), Hadfield et al. (2009), Valverde (2009), McCarthy (2014), McNamara and Quilter (2015), McCulloch and Wilson (2016), Crawford and Evans (2017).

[5]Crawford applies 'net-widening' to the use of Penalty Notices for Disorder (PNDs) in England and Wales, which police officers may impose for a range of disorderly behaviours (*Criminal Justice & Police Act 2001*, s1–11). Crawford asserts that up to three quarters of recipients of PNDs between 2004–06 would previously not have received any sort of formal sanction (2009, p. 821).

growth in the number of people subject to a formal criminal justice intervention. The expanding remit of discretionary and pre-emptive police powers applies primarily to lower level disorderly and anti-social behaviours, but this should not limit political or public concern about the potential effect of these mechanisms upon individual rights. As Zedner noted "both murderer and petty thief enjoy the same due process rights" (2005, p. 524). Within this broader context of the balance between issues of political expedience, public safety and individual rights, Victoria introduced its banning provisions. Banning notices target alcohol-related disorder in the NTE, and may be imposed for a specified offence, such as assault, or for more general anti-social acts and perceived nuisance, such as swearing. Banning notices address the types of low level behaviours that are increasingly subject to discretionary police punishment.

2.2 Discretionary Police Powers to Punish

Discretionary decisions are made across the criminal process, from pre-trial plea bargaining, witness selection and admission of evidence, to jury direction and sentencing (Findlay et al. 2010, p. 114). Police decisions, such as when to use force, or whether to warn, caution or arrest a suspect, are shaped by a range of legal, situational, interpretive, logistical, personal and pragmatic factors (Travis 1983). Policing is inherently and necessarily discretionary.[6] The use of discretion can be an effective and positive aspect of policing, but it is not always demonstrably fair, impartial or visible. Notable research into US, UK and Australian policing has explored the damaging consequences for procedural justice and police legitimacy of the way in which discretionary police powers, such as to move-on and stop/search, have been used disproportionately against certain racial groups.[7]

Legislative developments in many jurisdictions challenge the separation of powers within criminal justice processes. As members of the executive branch of government, police officers are increasingly called upon to determine guilt and administer justice summarily. Summary justice in this context refers specifically to the use of police-initiated pre-court punishments which dilute or circumvent established due process protections. The evolution of such provisions, from infringement penalties to banning notices, enables summary justice to be determined and imposed on-the-spot by police officers. This has significantly extended the reach of their discretionary powers, and

[6]Since the 1960s the definition and significance of police discretion and selective enforcement has been the focus of influential research. For example, Davis (1969, 1980), Klockars (1985), Finnane (1990), Skolnick (1994), Dixon (1997), Mastrofski (2004), Bronitt and Stenning (2011).

[7]For example, Weitzer and Tuch (2002), Weatherspoon (2004), Tyler and Wakslak (2004) Goodey (2006), Hallsworth (2006), Harris (2006), Walsh and Taylor (2007), Sivasubramaniam and Goodman-Delahunty (2008), Young (2010), Grossman et al. (2013), Yesufu (2013), Mazerolle et al. (2013), and Crawford et al. (2017). The issue of procedural justice and discriminatory policing is not a particular focus of this book, and this extensive body of research is not examined in detail.

is particularly evident in regulatory responses to public order issues in England and Wales, the USA, and Australia.

In the UK, the *Criminal Justice and Police Act 2001*, the *Anti-Social Behaviour Act 2003*, and the *Violent Crime Reduction Act 2006* introduced and extended Police Notices for Disorder (PNDs), dispersal orders and police exclusionary powers. PNDs carry financial penalties and are issued on-the-spot by police officers for a range of alcohol-related and disorderly behaviours. Dispersal orders enabled police officers to exclude recipients from designated areas for actual or perceived anti-social behaviours. Dispersal powers were revised in 2014. Section 34 of the *Anti-Social Behaviour, Crime and Policing Act* authorised the creation of dispersal zones and associated police powers to issue dispersal notices to individuals perceived to be likely to contribute to "harassment, alarm or distress" of the public. Such measures have facilitated a fundamental change in the role of police officers from law enforcers and investigators to both judge and jury as well. Beckett and Herbert (2008, 2009, 2010a, b) examined the use of police-imposed discretionary powers in Seattle, USA. Trespass rules allow police officers to issue on-the-spot exclusion orders from public spaces, which can last for up to a year. There is no requirement to provide any evidence of wrongdoing, and restrictions apply to extensive geographical areas (Beckett and Herbert 2008, 2010a). Such programs continue to grow and progressively increase the likelihood of infringement and punishment.

A similar move towards summary justice is evident in Australia. Fox and Freiberg (1989) discussed the growth of discretion afforded to the police in Victoria through the use of on-the-spot fines and infringement notices.[8] In Victoria, the number of actions and behaviours subject to police regulation and control continues to grow. Between 2006–7 and 2015–16, infringement notices issued by Victoria Police increased by nearly 35% to 3.1 million (Attorney-General, Victoria 2016, p. 9).

Discretion plays a key role in the imposition of summary justice by police officers. It is recognised that discretionary police decision-making is not inevitably problematic. However, police powers to punish risk the creation of a fundamental imbalance of rights, whereby the due process protections of the accused are subordinated to expansive discretionary police powers (Farmer 2016, 2017a, b). Across Australia, research has highlighted concerns in relation to police-imposed discretionary summary justice. Spooner (2001) noted abuses in Queensland, with move-on decisions made by police officers based on subjective perceptions rather than demonstrable behaviours. Walsh and Taylor (2006, 2007) synthesised trends in police move-on practices in Queensland, and identified evidence of harassment by police officers. A Queensland Crime and Misconduct Commission (CMC)[9] report cautioned that misuse of police discretion poses a serious risk to public confidence and police legitimacy (CMC 2010). In New South Wales (NSW), recommendations by the NSW Ombudsman (1999) to introduce a clear code of practice to improve accountability in the application of police move-on powers were not implemented. McNamara and

[8]Infringement notices were first introduced in Victoria via the *Magistrates (Summary Proceedings) Act 1975*.

[9]The name was changed to the Crime and Corruption Commission (CCC) in 2014.

Quilter (2015) drew attention to the continued risk of discrimination in NSW through police responses to subjectively defined disorderly behaviours. In Victoria, the Office of Police Integrity (OPI) conducted a detailed review of discretionary police powers to stop and search. Their report noted the lack of appropriate transparency and accountability for police decision-making. The absence of oversight and review, and failure to meet the legislated reporting requirements due to inadequate data collection were highlighted as significant issues (OPI 2012, p. 7). A detailed examination of the Victorian infringement notice system also documented concerns with respect to police conformity with guidelines for their issue (Saunders et al. 2013, p. 31).

2.3 Pre-emptive Controls and Prohibitions

The boundaries of criminal, civil and regulatory law have become increasingly blurred by legislative developments that have expanded the use of police-imposed penalties, under the auspices of both punishment and control. A judicial hearing would require guilt to be proven beyond reasonable doubt, but discretionary summary justice allows police determination of both guilt and punishment. In the context of social control, the management of disorderly behaviour and the promotion of community safety, prohibitive measures such as banning notices and the Anti-Social Behaviour Order (ASBO) have proliferated.[10] ASBOs epitomised the blurring of criminal and civil boundaries, and the dilution of the separation of powers. They were "two-step prohibtions (TSPs)" (Von Hirsch and Simester 2006, p. 174) which combined prohibitive civil orders with criminal breach proceedings. As well as being a post-conviction disposal, an ASBO could be applied for by police, social landlords and other local authority bodies (*Crime and Disorder Act 1998* (UK) s1; *Police Reform Act 2002* (UK) s61), and imposed without conviction. ASBOs typically included prohibitive elements, such as not entering a defined geographical area, or not associating with named individuals. These actions in themselves are not criminal, but if undertaken when an ASBO was in place could lead to criminal prosecution. Limits embedded within the rule of law do not apply to prohibitions like ASBOs, as they are a future-focused community protective measure rather than a punishment for an actual offence (Ashworth 2004).

---

[10]ASBOs were introduced under the UK's *Crime and Disorder Act 1998*. Intended to be used to resolve neighbourhood disputes, the legislation was designed to tackle behaviour that "caused or was likely to cause harassment, alarm or distress to one or more persons not of the same household" (UK *Crime & Disorder Act 1998*, part 1), and envisaged to apply primarily to adults. However, ASBOs quickly became synonymous with young people (Burney 2002), although their success continues to be debated (Garrett 2007; Squires 2008; Crawford 2008, 2009; Burney 2009; Donoghue 2010; Hodgkinson and Tilley 2011). ASBOs were eventually superseded by Criminal Behaviour Orders (CBOs) under the *Anti-Social Behaviour, Crime and Policing Act 2014*. CBOs continue to operate under prohibitive principles, with criminal sanctions available for breaches.

Similar prohibitive orders across Australian jurisdictions pre-date the introduction of ASBOs. The *Crimes (Family Violence) Act 1987* (Vic)[11] empowered police to issue discretionary orders with a variety of prohibitive conditions, for example exclusion from specified addresses, breach of which could lead to criminal prosecution.[12] Prohibitive Behaviour Orders (PBOs) were introduced in Western Australia in 2010. Like ASBOs, PBOs prohibit lawful behaviours, such as being present in a particular place. Breach of any of the requirements constitutes a criminal offence—thereby effectively criminalising non-criminal behaviours (Crofts and Mitchell 2011; Crofts and Witzleb 2011). Prohibitive orders embody a fundamental loss of procedural safeguards,[13] and typify the principles of pre-crime and preventative justice. Pre-crime relates to the notion of preventing wrongdoing, controlling risk and pro-actively managing behaviours, by enabling a person's intentions to be presumed rather than waiting for actions to occur. Pre-crime and pre-emptive justice have been the subject of notable research and analysis.[14] Crawford presents pre-crime as "directing and influencing prospective behaviour rather than reordering and accounting for past conduct" (2009, p. 814). Pre-crime and preventive justice continue to transform criminal justice processes and priorities, from individual responsibility and punishment towards the management of probability and risk. Traditional reactive, post hoc criminal processes are "mutated" (Hallsworth and Lea 2011, p. 146) by pre-emptive and preventive criminalisation.

Within this context, strategies developed in response to serious crime have increasingly been applied to lower level crime control under the banner of common sense. In Victoria, pre-punishment mechanisms had previously been directed towards serious risks to public safety from, for example, sex offenders[15] or the post-9/11 terror threat.[16] Discretionary police banning powers lowered the threshold to include prospective public disorder in the NTE. Within this preventive framework, individual rights and protections remain but their application is quietly diluted. The temporal shift inherent in the move from a post-crime, reactive focus towards pre-emptive management fundamentally challenges the traditional model of dealing with criminal behaviours, and the separation of powers (Rodger 2008a, b). Intent can be assumed merely from being present in a location. Once the notion of pre-emptive control is

---

[11]Superseded by the *Family Violence Protection Act 2008*.

[12]Under Victoria's *Crimes (Family Violence) Act 1987* (s23) police were able to impose an Intervention Order, and initiate an arrest for alleged breaches without a warrant.

[13]Due process rights that would be assured via summary prosecution (such as the presumption of innocence) are removed.

[14]For example, Feeley and Simon (1992), Fitzgibbon (2004), Tonry (2004), Pratt et al. (2005), Zedner (2007c), Rodger (2008a, b), Pantazis (2008), Crawford (2009), Van Wijck (2011), Hallsworth and Lea (2011), Ashworth and Zedner (2015), McCulloch and Wilson (2016).

[15]Victoria's *Serious Sex Offenders Monitoring Act 2005* authorised extended supervision for serious sex offenders after release from prison, in the interests of community protection.

[16]The *Anti-Terrorism Act 2005* (Cth) introduced Control Orders and Preventative Detention Orders. In New South Wales, the *Terrorism (Police Powers) Amendment (Investigative Detention) Act 2016*, authorised detention for up to 14 days without charge, and similar powers were proposed in Victoria during 2017.

established, the risk exists of it being applied more broadly to actions and behaviours only remotely related to crime. This is exemplified by the range of permissible provisions embodied within measures such as ASBOs, SODA orders, and PBOs. UK dispersal notices and Victoria's banning notices take this a step further, as each may be imposed entirely pre-emptively, according to the subjective assessment of a police officer.

Early interventions, risk assessments and preventive measures offer fundamental challenges to traditional principles of criminal justice, including the presumption of innocence and protections afforded by judicial review. The language of control, protection, prevention and enforcement allows established legal protections to be pushed aside, while in many cases failing to address or measure the effectiveness of interventions (Ashworth 2004; Crawford 2009). This is exemplified by O'Malley's depiction of the monetisation of justice (2009, 2010, 2011), whereby money, risk and justice converge. Administrative instruments, typified by infringement fines for traffic offences, enable simulated summary justice to operate generally outside of traditional judicial mechanisms. Both the risk and consequence are calculable and as long as the fine is paid, regardless of culpability or intent, then the risk is mitigated and justice served. O'Malley (2009) observed the progression of this monetised approach into non-traffic related forms of offending, such as disorderly behaviours. This enables police discretion to be enhanced and justice to be administered through on-the-spot executive action. Guilt is presumed, unless an appeal is lodged by the recipient, and justice occurs almost invisibly, with speed and efficiency.

The emphasis upon preventing undesirable behaviours, manifested in the literature of pre-emptive justice, is predicated on the assumption that the state can and should regulate such behaviours. Extending Garland's (2001) responsibilisation thesis, behaviours are regarded as the personal choices of individuals. Yet, there is a lack of objectivity in key constructs of criminality, and fluidity around what may be regarded as criminal behaviours. The actions that may lead to the imposition of various orders, admonishments and punishments are often vaguely defined and may not necessarily pass an appropriate threshold of criminality. Terms such as anti-social, quarrelsome and troublemaker are used in relation to Victoria's banning provisions, but what they mean in an objective or measurable sense is unclear. In the context of the rise of police-imposed summary justice and the lack of visibility and accountability regarding how and why such decisions are made, there is an absence of clarity regarding the definition and interpretation of behaviours that are subject to increasing police discretion. Victoria's banning provisions empower police officers to set their own precedents for behavioural thresholds and determinations of guilt.

2.4 Human Rights, Criminal Justice and 'Balance'

The increasing use of discretionary summary justice and pre-emptive controls are a reflection of, and a response to, changing political and operational pressures within a generally expanding body of criminal law. Clear procedures frame the functioning of criminal justice processes, ideally ensuring consistency, transparency, accountability, and effective separation of powers to uphold individual rights. However, legislative, regulatory and operational developments have expanded discretionary police powers and conflated previously distinct elements of the criminal process. Mechanisms such as infringement penalties and banning notices empower police officers to act as investigator, judge and jury. Criminal justice processes have evolved in response to changing expectations and pressures, in particular the prioritisation of community safety and national security.

A renewed focus on national and international human rights declarations and conventions, over the last four decades or so, has attempted to formalise due process protections for those accused of crimes.[17] Despite the emerging interplay of human rights charters and a more rights-focused conception of the criminal process, significant legislative developments demonstrate a 're-balancing' of the criminal process from the perceived primacy of defendants' rights towards the increasingly acknowledged needs of victims and communities more generally.[18] Manifestations of balance[19] are problematic, and are epitomised by the growth of discretionary police powers to punish. This creates an ambiguity as balance is skewed to embody inter-related assertions and expectations, with complex and potentially unknown consequences. Balance manifests across the breadth of criminal law. Re-balancing is evident in widespread state-imposed restrictions on liberty under the auspices of national security, through 'tough on crime'[20] reforms in the realm of law and order, and within Victoria's implementation of localised responses to address alcohol-related issues in the night-time economy.

Legislative changes and operational policing initiatives increasingly frame balance in terms of security and community rights, and typically reflect a drive by governments to be seen to respond to specific issues. The underpinning discourse tends to promote divisions between them and us, and positions the balancing responses as being in the interests of 'us' as the wider community. Significantly, the presumed needs of the public at large are prioritised and any effect upon the rights of 'them', the undesirable minority, are generally ignored. Legislative developments increasingly

---

[17]The Bill of Rights amendments to the US *Constitution 1791*, the UN *Universal Declaration of Human Rights 1948*, the *European Convention on Human Rights 1950*, and the UN *ICCPR 1966*, set the scene for a renewed focus upon formal human rights conventions in recent decades. Key examples include the Canadian *Charter of Rights and Freedoms 1982*, the New Zealand *Human Rights Act 1993*, South African *Bill of Rights 1996*, UK *Human Rights Act 1998*, *Charter of Fundamental Rights of the European Union 2000*, ACT *Human Rights Act 2004*, Victoria's *Charter of Human Rights and Responsibilities 2006*. At a Federal level in Australia, the Commonwealth Parliamentary Joint Committee on Human Rights (established by the *Human Rights (Parliamentary Scrutiny) Act 2011*), oversees human rights compliance.

[18]Re-balancing, while evident across key legislative provisions, has been comprehensively challenged within a significant body of literature. For example, Ashworth (1996), Zedner (2002, 2003, 2005, 2007a, b, 2014), Waldron (2003), Tonry (2003, 2010), Michaelsen (2005, 2006, 2010), Neocleous (2007), Williams (2007a, b), Bronitt (2008), Pue (2008) and others.

[19]While acknowledging the issues inherent in the application of balance, Williams (2006, 2007a, b) specifically recognises the convenience of the balance metaphor as a means to facilitate dialogue.

[20]Tony Blair first used the phrase "tough on crime and tough on the causes of crime" during his first speech to the Labour Party as its new leader (Blair 1994).

position the broader community as the primary, if prospective, victim (Farmer 2017b). The expansion of discretionary, pre-emptive provisions are justified, therefore, in the interests of public protection, political expediency, community safety and the promotion of proactive governance. The consequences of measures to 're-balance' are tangible. Changes to the criminal process and the expansion of discretionary police powers reduce the rights of those either accused of crime or perceived to be intent on undesirable behaviours.

2.5 Security, Risk Mitigation and Community Protection

Legislative and operational provisions are increasingly predicated upon a need to ensure the security and safety of the community, and driven by a desire to be seen do something about high profile issues (Ashworth 2006b; Crawford 2013). Government policy limiting individual rights should be supported by empirical evidence of both the need and effectiveness. The expectation of evidence-based policy development in Victoria is stated explicitly within the *Charter Act 2006* (s.7(2)). Although in the context of responses to 9/11, Waldron (2003) asserted that the 'means' and the 'ends' of legislative and operational provisions must not be confused. He contended that hardening the response to crime, by prioritising the security of the majority over the rights of the minority who are perceived as a risk, does not necessarily make the majority safer. There are clear parallels with alcohol-related disorder in the NTE, where the desire to expand discretionary police powers to punish is justified by the expected outcome of increased community safety. What happens if the means do not have the expected effect, or if the underlying need is not sufficient to justify the means, are typically not the focus of concern. States are resorting to what Neocleous (2007, p. 146) referred to as the "anti-politics of 'security-trumps'" to validate growing restrictions on liberty across a range of contexts, against which any opposition is problematic and can lead to accusations of undermining national security or public safety. In this context, the myth of balance, therefore, enables a move towards more authoritarian measures that erode individual rights (Farmer 2017a, b).

Assertions of necessity increasingly determines legislative responses, and enables governments to legitimise changes to police powers which lack a basis in evidence, but which create an impression of proactive and strong governance (Caplow and Simon 1999; Garland 2001; Tonry 2003, 2010; Crawford 2009). There is likely to be little political, media or public opposition when being tough is promoted as an essential response to a significant if unquantified risk, and combines with a robust parliamentary majority. Despite the expectations formalised within frameworks such as the *Charter Act*, political expedience enables effective scrutiny to be circumvented and augments the inefficacy of re-balancing (Farmer 2017a, b).

The discourse of security and community protection reflects an expanding notion of victimisation, and recent changes in the criminal process have served to broaden its depiction. Increasingly pre-emptive responses to perceived risks have extended the remit of prospective victimisation to include the wider community as a whole.

New legislative provisions and operational police powers are justified with reference to the needs of public protection. A prominent early example are reforms introduced in the UK from the mid 1990s under the 'tough on crime' mantra.[21] They typify fundamental changes to the balance of the criminal process via police-imposed, pre-emptive and/or prohibitive provisions, such as ASBOs and dispersal orders. The single priority expressed in the White Paper 'Justice for All' epitomises the direction being taken.

> … to re-balance the criminal justice system in favour of the victims and the community so as to reduce crime and bring more offenders to justice. (Home Office (UK) 2003, p. 5)

However, rights should not be regarded as obstacles in the criminal process (Ashworth 1996). Giving due attention to the rights of all parties should not result in underlying issues, such as national security or community safety, being neglected. Public accountability is essential to uphold rights, via mechanisms to challenge discretionary decisions and to review the effect upon criminal processes. Individual due process rights and community safety are not mutually exclusive.

Defending limitations on the rights of individuals, in the broader interests of the community, brings into question the place of the affected individuals within that community (Waldron 2003). This concern is of direct relevance to the consequences of police-imposed summary justice. Discretionary police powers have shifted the balance within criminal justice processes in favour of victims and the broader community, and diluted the separation of powers. In this context, the individual rights of the undesirable minority are undermined and subordinated to the rights of the majority (Farmer 2017a, b).

2.6 Balancing Need, Risk and Individual Rights

The undermining or removal of due process rights must be "proportionate to the risks faced" (Zedner 2007c, p. 266). If new summary police powers are permitted to dilute due process protections, based upon promises of increased safety or crime reduction, both the underlying need and the ongoing effect of the response must be measurable and monitored.[22] The justification for the expansion of discretionary pre-emptive police powers is typically predicated upon notions of protection, and a concomitant desire to re-balance the needs of the broader community away from the disorderly and troublesome minority. In themselves these are objectives that are difficult to counter. However, Victoria's banning notice provisions embody a clear and potentially troubling dichotomy (Farmer 2017a, b). Political rhetoric typically emphasises the need for security or community safety in order to legitimise measures

[21] Specific legislative measures such as the *Crime and Disorder Act 1998*, *Police Reform Act 2002*, *Criminal Justice and Court Services Act 2002*, *Criminal Justice Act 2003* and the *Anti-Social Behaviour Act 2003*, have been subject to extensive analysis.

[22] This aligns with broader expectations of evidence-based policing, policy and practice (Sherman 1998; MacCoun 2005; Bradford et al. 2014).

that dilute individual rights, but too often the nature and extent of the actual risk is not tested and the effect of the new provisions are not monitored. Assertions of need, whether genuine or perceived, generate public fear and a resulting determination, by incumbent Governments, to respond. The perceived urgency of the need to act enables effective scrutiny of the proposed provisions to be circumvented. When such a combination of events results in individual rights being undermined by increasing police powers, that are not subject to meaningful review, and which may not address the need that has been asserted, a clear risk to due process is created. When individuals cannot seek a meaningful independent review of the discretionary police powers to punish, such as banning notices, the risk to individual rights and to the provision of justice are increased. An absence of scrutiny reinforces the need for effective pre-enactment assessment of legislative proposals which expand police powers and limit individual rights, to ensure that the need is verified, and the response is monitored.

Balance is increasingly evident within policy decisions in relation to a perceived need to protect the broader community (Farmer 2017a, b). However, while re-asserting the rights of actual and prospective victims, both individual and collective, the due process protections for alleged offenders or individuals regarded as undesirable are eroded. The drive to re-balance risks expanding the reach of victimisation to include individuals who are subjected to pre-emptive, prohibitive and increasingly expansive discretionary police powers to punish, and who are denied both legal support and any right of independent review.

In Victoria, the *Charter Act* comprises detailed procedures to ensure legislative and operational conformance with the purpose of its provisions. However, the Charter protections are not absolute and the Victorian Parliament is empowered to circumvent the proscribed human rights.[23] While a clear and comprehensive process is set out within the *Charter Act*, legislative provisions that restrict individual rights, such as banning notices, can be legitimised first by the subjective determination of politicians, then by the perceptions of police officers. The *Charter Act,* that should ensure open accountability for the rights of citizens, can be circumvented by the government. This creates a structural weakness, challenges the rule of law, and undermines human rights. The passage of Victoria's *Charter Act* and its application of rights to the development of legislation embodies the notion of 'law in books, law in action' (Pound 1910; Halperin 2011). Despite a proliferation of human rights mechanisms, the formal assertion of rights is disconnected from their implementation (Farmer 2017a).[24] More specifically, Valverde (2009) observes that charters and conventions appear to carry little weight in relation to low-level disorder, and notes that localised discretionary police powers are rarely considered in the context of human rights.

[23]For example, Charter rights may be subject to reasonable limitations, which must be empirically justified (*Charter Act 2006*, s7(2)). In "exceptional circumstances" (s31(4)), an override declaration may be invoked.

[24]See, for example, Hiebert (1998, 2005, 2012), Hathaway (2002, 2007), Feldman (2002, 2004), Goodman and Jinks (2003), Landman (2004), Waldron (2005), Williams (2006, 2007a, b), Golder and Williams (2007), Hafner-Burton and Tsutsui (2007), Gearty (2009), Valverde (2009), Simmons (2009), Sandtow (2010), Evans and Evans (2006, 2011), Horrigan (2012), Rodgers (2012), Cole (2013), Cole and Ramirez (2013), and Rares (2013).

Victoria's banning notice provisions highlight the effect and normative significance of the move to summary justice, and the importance of the way in which discretionary powers are afforded to police officers. Banning notices embody a fundamental challenge to the traditional liberal model of criminal justice, whereby clear procedural safeguards for the accused sit within a process that provides open and appropriate justice (Ashworth and Zedner 2008). Within a growing body of criminal law, and reflecting a combination of drivers and perceived issues with established models of criminal justice, legislation targeting undesirable behaviours increasingly circumvents the criminal law and side-steps the individual rights of defendants. In the antithetical context of the re-balancing agenda and the formalisation of human rights in the scrutiny of legislative provisions, the resolution of such divergent drivers is problematic. Even under Victoria's *Charter Act*, human rights are not assured and the Victorian Parliament may pass legislation in contravention of key rights. That legislation can circumvent provisions which should protect individual rights, such as Victoria's *Charter Act*, in the interests of loosely framed public protection is concerning. The LCRA Bill 2007 was passed in the first year of the Charter's operation. Given the due process and human rights issues embedded within the banning provisions, the enactment of the legislation raises concerns about the implementation of the Charter compliance requirements, and the process of parliamentary scrutiny as a whole. The justifying rationale and the way in which parliamentary processes were applied enabled the banning provisions to be introduced through the *LCRA Act 2007*, and extended under the *JLA Act 2010,* despite significant consequences for individual rights that should be protected by the Charter. The banning notice provisions circumvented the *Charter Act* to legitimise discretionary police powers that then circumvent individual rights.

The broader consequences of the growth of discretionary police powers to punish are essentially unknown, due largely to an absence of empirical analysis. Victoria's police-imposed banning notices were enacted to 're-balance' the provision of justice in the NTE, to prioritise the collective needs of community protection and legitimise the dilution of individual due process rights. However, when driven by political expedience and fear, rather than public scrutiny, the potential futility of the notion of re-balancing is significant. The next chapter provides an overview of Victoria's banning notice provisions, then sets out the research method which underpins the subsequent examination of the rationale for banning and the post-enactment scrutiny of the police power to ban.

References

Ashworth, A. (1996, April). Crime, community and creeping consequentialism. *Criminal Law Review,* 220–230.

Ashworth, A. (2004). Social control and 'anti-social behaviour': The subversion of human rights? *Law Quarterly Review, 120,* 263–291.

Ashworth, A. (2006a). Four threats to the presumption of innocence. *The International Journal of Evidence and Proof, 10,* 241–279.

Ashworth, A. (2006b). *Principles of criminal law* (5th ed.). Oxford: Oxford University Press.
Ashworth, A., & Zedner, L. (2008). Defending the criminal law: Reflections on the changing character of crime, procedure and sanctions. *Criminal Law and Philosophy, 2,* 21–51.
Ashworth, A., & Zedner, L. (2015). *Preventive justice*. Oxford: Oxford University Press.
Attorney-General, Victoria. (2016). *Annual report on the infringements system 2010–2011*. Victoria: Department of Justice.
Australian Human Rights Commission (AHRC). (no date). *International covenant on civil and political rights—Human rights at your fingertips—Human rights at your fingertips.* [Online]: AHRC. Retrieved from https://www.humanrights.gov.au/international-covenant-civil-and-political-rights-human-rights-your-fingertips-human-rights-your.
Bateman, W. (2009). Procedural due process under the Australian constitution. *Sydney Law Review, 31,* 411–442.
Beckett, K., & Herbert, S. (2008). Dealing with disorder: Social control in the post-industrial city. *Theoretical Criminology, 12*(1), 5–30.
Beckett, K., & Herbert, S. (2009). Zoning out disorder: Assessing contemporary practices of urban social control. *New Perspectives on Crime and Criminal Justice, 47,* 1–25.
Beckett, K., & Herbert, S. (2010a). *Banished. The new social control in Urban America*. New York: Oxford University Press.
Beckett, K., & Herbert, S. (2010b). Penal boundaries; banishment and the expansion of punishment. *Law & Social Inquiry, 35*(1), 1–38.
Blair, T. (1994). *Leader's speech.* Presented at the Labour Party Conference, Blackpool, UK.
Blake, M., & Ashworth, A. (1996). The presumption of innocence in English criminal law. *Criminal Law Review,* 306–317.
Bradford, B., Murphy, K., & Jackson, J. (2014). Officers as mirrors. *British Journal of Criminology, 54,* 527–550.
British Library. (no date). *Magna Carta.* [translation of original text]. [Online]: British Library. Retrieved from http://www.bl.uk/magna-carta/articles/magna-carta-english-translation.
Bronitt, S. (2008). Balancing security and liberty: Critical perspectives on terrorism law reform. In M. Gani & P. Mathew (Eds.), *Fresh perspectives on the 'war on terror'* (pp. 65–84). Canberra: ANU.
Bronitt, S., & Stenning, P. (2011). Understanding discretion in modern policing. *Criminal Law Journal, 35,* 319–332.
Burney, E. (2002). Talking tough, acting coy: What happened to the anti-social behaviour order? *The Howard Journal, 41,* 469–484.
Burney, E. (2009). *Making people behave: Anti-social behaviour, policy and politics*. Cullompton, Devon: Willan Publishing.
Caplow, T., & Simon, J. (1999). Understanding prison policy and population trends. *Berkeley Law Scholarship Repository, 1*(1), 63–120.
Castles, A. C. (1982). *An Australian legal history*. Sydney: Law Book Company Limited.
Cole, W. M. (2013). Strong walk and cheap talk: The effect of the international covenant of economic, social and cultural rights on policies and practices. *Social and Economic Rights in Law and Practice, 92*(1), 165–194.
Cole, W. M., & Ramirez, F. O. (2013). Conditional decoupling: Assessing the impact of national human rights institutions, 1981 to 2004. *American Sociological Review, 78*(4), 702–725.
Crawford, A. (2008). Dispersal powers and the symbolic role of anti-social behaviour legislation. *Modern Law Review, 71*(5), 753–784.
Crawford, A. (2009). Governing through anti-social behaviour: regulatory challenges to criminal justice. *British Journal of Criminology, 49*(6), 810–831.
Crawford, A. (2013). 'Sticks and carrots and sermons': Some thoughts on compliance and legitimacy in the regulation of youth anti-social behaviour. In A. Crawford & A. Hucklesby (Eds.), *Legitimacy and compliance in criminal justice* (pp. 181–214). Abingdon, Oxon: Routledge.

Crawford, A., & Evans, K. (2017). Crime prevention and community safety. In A. Leibling, S. Maruna, & L. McAra (Eds.), *The oxford handbook of criminology* (6th ed.). Oxford: Oxford University Press.

Crawford, A., Lewis, S., & Traynor, P. (2017). 'It ain't (just) what you do, it's (also) the way that you do it': The role of procedural justice in the implementation of anti-social behaviour interventions with young people. *European Journal on Criminal Policy and Research, 23*(1), 9–26.

Crime and Misconduct Commission (CMC). (2010). *Police move-on powers: a CMC review of their use*. Brisbane: Crime and Misconduct Commission.

Crofts, T., & Mitchell, T. (2011). Prohibited behaviour orders and indigenous overrepresentation in the criminal justice system. *Current Issues in Criminal Justice, 23*(2), 277–285.

Crofts, T., & Witzleb, N. (2011). 'Naming and Shaming' in Western Australia: Prohibited behaviour orders, publicity and the decline of youth anonymity. *Criminal Law Journal, 35*(1), 34–45.

Davis, K. C. (1969). *Discretionary justice*. Baton Rouge: Louisiana State University Press.

Davis, K. C. (1980). *Discretionary justice: A preliminary inquiry* (Reprint ed.). London: Greenwood Press.

Dixon, D. (1997). *Law in policing: Legal regulation and police practices*. Oxford: Clarendon Press.

Donoghue, J. (2010). *Anti-social behaviour orders: A culture of control?*. Basingstoke: Palgrave MacMillan.

Evans, C., & Evans, S. (2006). Legislative scrutiny committees and parliamentary conceptions on human rights. *Public Law,* (Winter), 785–806.

Evans, C., & Evans, S. (2011). Messages from the front line: Parliamentarians' perspectives on rights protection. In K. D. Ewing & A. Tomkins (Eds.), *The legal protection of human rights: Sceptical essays* (pp. 329–346). Oxford: Oxford University Press.

Farmer, C. (2014). Is a 24-hour ban such a bad thing? *Australian Journal of Human Rights, 20*(2), 39–62.

Farmer, C. (2016). Victoria's banning notice provisions: Parliamentary, procedural and individual vulnerabilities. *Journal of Criminological Research, Policy & Practice, 2*(3), 173–184.

Farmer, C. (2017a). The disparity between human rights policy and parliamentary practice in Australia: A Victorian case study. *The International Journal of Human Rights, 27*(2), 167–188.

Farmer, C. (2017b). Upholding whose right? Discretionary police powers to punish, collective 'pre-victimisation' and the dilution of individual rights. *Australian & New Zealand Journal of Criminology, 50*(4), 493–509.

Feeley, M. M., & Simon, J. (1992). The new penology: Notes on the emerging strategy of corrections and its implications. *Criminology, 30*(4), 449–474.

Feldman, D. (2002). Parliamentary scrutiny of legislation and human rights. *Public Law, 2,* 323–348.

Feldman, D. (2004). The impact of human rights on the UK legislative process. *Statute Law Review, 25*(2), 91–115.

Findlay, M., Odgers, S., & Yeo, S. (2010). *Australian criminal justice* (4th ed.). Sydney: Oxford University Press.

Findley, K. A. (2009). Toward a new paradigm of criminal justice: How the innocence movement merges crime control and due process. *Texas Law Review, Research Paper No. 1069.*

Finnane, M. (1990). Police and politics in Australia: The case for historical revision. *Australian & New Zealand Journal of Criminology, 23*(4), 218–228.

Fitzgibbon, D. W. (2004). *Pre-emptive criminalisation: Risk control and alternative futures*. London: NAPO.

French, R. (2009). *The constitution and the protection of human rights*. Edith Cowan University Vice-Chancellor's Oration, Perth. [Online]. Retrieved from http://www.hcourt.gov.au/assets/publications/speeches/current-justices/frenchcj/frenchcj20nov09.pdf.

Fox, R., & Freiberg, A. (1989). Sentences without Conviction: from status to contract in sentencing. *Criminal Law Journal, 13*, 297–323.

Galligan, D. J. (1996). *Due process and fair procedures: A study of administrative procedures*. Oxford: Clarendon Press.

Garland, D. (2001). *The culture of control: Crime and social order in contemporary society*. Oxford: Oxford University Press.

Garrett, P. M. (2007). Making 'anti-social behaviour': A fragment on the evolution of 'ASBO politics' in Britain. *British Journal of Social Work, 37,* 839–856.

Gearty, C. (2009). Human rights in and age of counter-terrorism. In C. Miller (Ed.), *'War on terror' The oxford amnesty lectures 2006* (pp. 83–98). Manchester: Manchester University Press.

Golder, B., & Williams, G. (2007). Balancing national security and human rights: Assessing the legal response of common law nations to the threat of terrorism. *Journal of Comparative Policy Analysis: Research and Practice, 8*(1), 43–62.

Goodey, J. (2006). Ethnic profiling, criminal (in) justice and minority populations. *Critical Criminology, 14,* 207–212.

Goodman, R., & Jinks, D. (2003). Measuring the effects of human rights treaties. *European Journal of International Law, 14*(1), 171–183.

Grossman, M., Bruck, D., Stephenson, P., Dwyer, R., & Roose, J. (2013). *Learning to engage: A review of Victoria police cross-cultural training practices*. Melbourne: Victoria University.

Hadfield, P., Lister, S., & Traynor, P. (2009). 'This town's a different town today': Policing and regulating the night-time economy. *Criminology & Criminal Justice: An International Journal, 9*(4), 465–485.

Hafner-Burton, E. M., & Tsutsui, K. (2007). Justice lost! The failure of international human rights law to matter where needed most. *Journal of Peace Research, 44*(4), 407–425.

Hallsworth, S. (2006). Racial targeting and social control: Looking behind the police. *Critical Criminology, 14*(3), 293–311.

Hallsworth, S., & Lea, J. (2011). Reconstructing Leviathan: Emerging contours of the security state. *Theoretical Criminology, 15*(2), 141–157.

Halperin, J.-L. (2011). Law in books and law in action: The problem of legal change. *Maine Law Review, 64*(1), 46–76.

Harris, D. A. (2006). US experiences with racial and ethnic profiling: History, current issues and the future. *Critical Criminology, 14*(3), 213–239.

Hathaway, O. (2002). Do human rights treaties make a difference? *Yale Law Journal, 112,* 1935–2042.

Hathaway, O. (2007). Why do countries commit to human rights treaties? *Journal of Conflict Resolution, 51*(4), 588–621.

Hiebert, J. L. (1998). A hybrid approach to protect rights? An argument in favour of supplementing Canadian judicial review with Australia's model of parliamentary scrutiny. *Federal Law Review, 26,* 115–138.

Hiebert, J. L. (2005). Interpreting a bill of rights: The importance of legislative rights review. *British Journal of Political Science, 35*(2), 235–255.

Hiebert, J. L. (2012). Parliamentary engagement wit the charter: Rethinking the idea of legislative rights review. *Supreme Court Law Review, 58,* 87–107.

Hodgkinson, S., & Tilley, N. (2011). Tackling anti-social behaviour: Lessons from new labour for the coalition government. *Criminology & Criminal Justice, 11*(4), 283–305.

Home Office (UK). (2003). *Respect and responsibility: Taking a stand against anti-social behaviour*. London: Home Office.

Horrigan, B. (2012). Reforming rights-based scrutiny and interpretation of legislation. *Alternative Law Journal, 37*(4), 228–232.

Keon-Cohen, B. A. (1991). *Can the Victorian Parliament abolish fundamental rights?* Paper presented at the AIC Sentencing, Psychiatry and Law Reform Conference, Melbourne.

Keyzer, P. (2008). Preserving due process or warehousing the undesirables: To what end the separation of judicial power of the Commonwealth? *Sydney Law Review, 30,* 101–114.

Klockars, C. B. (1985). *The idea of police*. Beverly Hills, CA: Sage Publications.

Landman, T. (2004). Measuring human rights: Principle, policy, and practice. *Human Rights Quarterly, 26,* 906–931.

Lord Irvine of Lairg. (2002). *The spirit of the Magna Carta continues to resonate in modern law*. The Inaugural Magna Carta Lecture, Canberra: [Online]. Retrieved from https://www.aph.gov.au/binaries/senate/pubs/pops/pop39/lairg.pdf.
MacCoun, R. J. (2005). Voice, control and belonging: the double-edge sword of procedural fairness. *Annual Review of Law and Social Science, 1,* 171–201.
Mastrofski, S. D. (2004). Controlling street-level police discretion. *American Academy of Political and Social Science, 593*(1), 100–118.
Mazerolle, L., Bennett, S., Davis, J., Sargeant, E., & Manning, M. (2013). Legitimacy in policing: A systematic review. *Campbell Systematic Reviews, 1,* 1–146.
McCarthy, D. (2014). *'Soft' policing: The collaborative control of anti-social behaviour*. London: Palgrave.
McCulloch, J., & Wilson, D. J. (2016). *Pre-crime: Pre-emption, precaution and the future*. Abingdon, Oxon: Routledge.
McNamara, L. J., & Quilter, J. (2015). Public intoxication in NSW: The contours of criminalisation. *The Sydney Law Review, 37*(1), 1–35.
Michaelsen, C. (2005). Antiterrorism legislation in Australia: A proportionate response to the terrorist threat? *Studies in Conflict and Terrorism, 28*(4), 321.
Michaelsen, C. (2006). Balancing civil liberties against national security? A critique of counterterrorism rhetoric. *UNSW Law Journal, 29*(2), 1–21.
Michaelsen, C. (2010). The proportionality principle, counter-terrorism laws and human rights: A German-Australian comparison. *City University of Hong Kong Law Review, 2*(1), 19–43.
Neocleous, M. (2007). Security, liberty and the myth of balance: Towards a critique of security politics. *Contemporary Political Theory, 6,* 131–149.
New South Wales (NSW) Ombudsman. (1999). *Policing public safety*. Sydney: NSW Ombudsman.
Office of Police Integrity (OPI). (2012). *Review of Victoria police use of 'stop and search' powers*. Melbourne: Office of Police Integrity.
O'Malley, P. (2009). Theorising fines. *Punishment & Society, 11,* 67–83.
O'Malley, P. (2010). Simulated justice: Risk, money and telemetric policing. *British Journal of Criminology, 50,* 795–807.
O'Malley, P. (2011). The currency of freedom? *Social & Legal Studies, 20*(4), 546–556.
Pantazis, C. (2008). The problem with criminalisation. *Criminal Justice Matters, 74*(1), 10–12.
Parliament of Australia. (n.d.). *Parliamentary joint committee on human rights*. [Online]: Parliament of Australia. Retrieved from http://www.aph.gov.au/Parliamentary_Business/Committees/Joint/Human_Rights.
Pound, R. (1910). Law in books and law in action. *American Law Review, 44,* 12–36.
Pratt, J., Brown, D., Brown, M., Hallsworth, S., & Morrison, W. (2005). *The new punitiveness: Trends, theories and perspectives*. Collompton, Devon: Willan Publishing.
Pue, W. W. (2008). Protecting constitutionalism in treacherous times: Why 'rights' don't matter. In M. Gani & P. Mathew (Eds.), *Fresh perspectives on the 'War on terror'* (pp. 45–64). Canberra: ANU.
Rares, S. (2013). *Legality, rights and statutory interpretation*. Paper presented at the AGS Administrative Law Conference, Canberra.
Rodger, J. R. (2008a). *Criminalising social policy: Anti social behaviour and welfare in a decivilised society*. Collompton, Devon: Willan Publishing.
Rodger, J. R. (2008b). The criminalisation of social policy. *Criminal Justice Matters, 74*(1), 18–19.
Rodgers, C. (2012). A comparative analysis of rights scrutiny in New Zealand, Australia and the United Kingdom: Is New Zealand lagging behind its peers? *Australasian Parliamentary Review, 27*(1), 4–17.
Sandtow, E. (2010). *Enhanced scrutiny of rights: Of parliament, pigs and lipstick*. Paper presented at the AIAL National Administrative Law Forum, Sydney.
Saunders, B., Eriksson, A., Lansdell, G., & Brown, M. (2013). *An examination of the impact of unpaid infringement notices on disadvantaged groups and the criminal justice system—Towards a best practice model Criminal Justice Research Consortium*. Melbourne: Monash University.

Sherman, L. W. (1998). *Evidence-based policing. Ideas on American policing*. Washington DC: Police Foundation.
Simmons, B. (2009). *Mobilising for human rights: International law and domestic enforcement*. New York: Cambridge University Press.
Sivasubramaniam, D., & Goodman-Delahunty, J. (2008). Ethnicity and trust: Perceptions of police bias. *International Journal of Police Sciences & Management, 10,* 388–440.
Skolnick, J. H. (1994). *Justice without trial: Law enforcement in democratic society* (3rd ed.). New York: MacMillan Publishing.
Spigelman, J. (2008). Statutory interpretation and human rights: McPherson lecture series. *University of Queensland Press, 3,* 1–49.
Spooner, P. (2001). 'Moving in the wrong direction': An analysis of police move-on powers in Queensland. *Youth Studies Australia, 20*(1), 27–31.
Squires, P. (2008). *ASBO Nation: The criminalisation of nuisance*. Bristol: The Policy Press.
Tonry, M. (2003). *Confronting crime: Crime control policy under new labour*. Abingdon, Oxon: Routledge.
Tonry, M. (2004). *Punishment and politics: Evidence and emulation in the making of English crime control policy*. Collompton, Devon: Willan Publishing.
Tonry, M. (2010). The costly consequences of populist posturing: ASBOs, victims, 'rebalancing' and diminution in support for civil liberties. *Punishment & Society, 12*(4), 387–413.
Travis, G. (1983). Police discretion in law enforcement: A study of section 5 of the NSW offences in public places act 1979. In M. Findlay, S. Egger, & J. Sutton (Eds.), *Issues in criminal justice administration* (pp. 200–219). Sydney: Allen & Unwin.
Tyler, T. R., & Wakslak, C. J. (2004). Profiling and police legitimacy: Procedural justice, attributions of motive, and acceptance of police authority. *Criminology, 42*(2), 253–281.
Valverde, M. (2009). Jurisdiction and scale: Legal 'technicalities' as resources for theory. *Social & Legal Studies, 18*(2), 139–157.
Van Wijck, P. (2011). The economics of pre-crime interventions. *European Journal of Law and Economics, 35*(3), 441–458.
Von Hirsch, A., & Simester, A. P. (2006). *Incivilities: Regulating offensive behaviour*. Oxford: Hart Publishing.
Waldron, J. (2003). Security and liberty: The image of balance. *The Journal of Political Philosophy, 11*(2), 191–210.
Waldron, J. (2005, December). Compared to what? Judicial activism and New Zealand's parliament. *New Zealand Law Journal,* 441–446.
Walker, G. de Q. (1988). *The rule of law: Foundation of constitutional democracy.* Melbourne: Melbourne University Press.
Walsh, T., & Taylor, M. (2006). *Nowhere to go: The impact of police move-on powers on homeless people in Queensland*. Brisbane: Queensland Public Interest Law Clearing House.
Walsh, T., & Taylor, M. (2007). 'You're not welcome here': Police move-on powers and discrimination law. *University of New South Wales Law Journal, 30,* 151–173.
Weatherpoon, F. D. (2004). Racial profiling of African-American Males: Stopped, Searched And Stripped Of Constitutional Protection. *The John Marshall Law Review, 38*(2), 439–468.
Weitzer, R., & Tuch, S. A. (2002). Perceptions of racial profiling: Race. *Class and Personal Experience. Criminology, 40*(2), 435–456.
Wheeler, F. (1997). The doctrine of separation of powers and constitutionally entrenched due process in Australia. *Monash University Law Review, 23*(2), 248–284.
Wheeler, F. (2004). Due process, judicial power and chapter III in the new high court. *Federal Law Review, 32,* 205–224.
Williams, G. (2006). The Victorian charter of human rights and responsibilities: Origins and scope. *Melbourne University Law Review, 30,* 880–905.
Williams, G. (2007a). Victoria's new charter: Human rights and the community. *Just Policy,* (43), 6–10.

Williams, G. (2007b, February). Lessons from Victoria's charter of human rights and responsibilities. *Law Society Journal,* 68–72.

Yesufu, S. (2013). Discriminatory use of police stop and search powers in London, UK. *International Journal of Police Sciences & Management, 15*(4), 281–293.

Young, R. (2010). Ethnic profiling and summary justice—An ominous silence. In K. Sveinsson (Ed.), *Ethnic profiling: The use of 'race' in UK law enforcement* (pp. 43–49). London: Runnymede Trust.

Zedner, L. (2002). Dangers of dystopias in penal theory (extended review of David Garland, The culture of control: Crime and social order in contemporary society). *Oxford Journal of Legal Studies, 22*(2), 341–366.

Zedner, L. (2003). Too much security? *International Journal of the Sociology of Law, 31*(3), 155–184.

Zedner, L. (2005). Securing liberty in the face of terror; reflections from criminal justice. *Journal of Law and Society, 32*(4), 507–533.

Zedner, L. (2007a). Preventive justice or pre-punishment? The case of control orders. *Current Legal Problems, 60*(1), 174–2003.

Zedner, L. (2007b). Seeking security by eroding rights: The side-stepping of due process. In B. Goold and L. Lazarus (Eds.), *Security and human rights* (pp. 257–275). Oxford: Hart Publishing.

Zedner, L. (2007c). Pre-crime and post-criminology? *Theoretical Criminology, 11*(2), 261–281.

Zedner, L. (2014). Terrorising criminal law. *Criminal Law and Philosophy, 8,* 99–121.

Chapter 3
Victoria's Banning Notice Provisions: A Case Study

Abstract This chapter sets out the case study of Victoria's banning notice legislation. The key operational components of banning notices are explained in the first part of the chapter. The research design and methodology from which the case study has been developed are then outlined. The third part of the chapter explores the arguments and rhetoric which underpinned the passage of the banning legislation: key assumptions are examined, parliamentary discourse is analysed, and consideration is given to the effect of the underlying presumptions and justifications upon the compliance requirements of Victoria's *Charter of Human Rights and Responsibilities Act 2006*. The final part of the chapter considers whether the claims made to justify the need for Victoria's banning provisions have been meaningfully tested: published banning notice data is examined, media coverage of banning and its use/effectiveness is analysed, and key findings from interview research with Victorian Magistrates are presented.

3.1 Overview of Victoria's Banning Notice Provisions[1]

Under the *Liquor Control Reform Amendment Act 2007* ('*LCRA Act 2007*') Victoria Police were given powers to exclude individuals from defined public areas, initially for 24 h. Victoria's banning notice provisions formed one component of a multi-dimensional response to concerns about issues of alcohol-related disorder in Victoria's night-time economy (NTE). A combination of legislative and operational policing measures were consolidated under Victoria's Alcohol Action Plan (Department of Justice 2008a).[2]

[1] This overview of victoria's banning notice legislation draws on earlier articles which have examined specific aspects of the provisions (Farmer 2014, 2016, 2017a, b).

[2] Notable measures include the creation of the Safe Streets task force, an operational policing initiative to increase the visible police presence in central Melbourne on Friday and Saturday nights.

C. Farmer, *Discretionary Police Powers to Punish*, SpringerBriefs in Criminology,
https://doi.org/10.1007/978-981-10-8869-8_3

To implement the banning provisions, the *LCRA Act 2007* empowered the then Director of Liquor Licensing[3] to declare a designated area if "alcohol-related violence or disorder has occurred in a public place that is in the immediate vicinity of licensed premises within the area" (s147(1a)), and if it was believed that banning notices would control or prevent further "alcohol related violence or disorder in the area" (s147(1b)). The "immediate vicinity" is defined as a "place that is within 100 metres of the licensed premises" (s147(3)). Victoria's first two designated areas were declared in December 2007, and covered the Melbourne Central Business District (CBD) and Prahran/South Yarra, incorporating the Chapel Street area of inner Melbourne (VCGLR 2017). Additional entertainment precincts in Metropolitan Melbourne and all major regional centres across Victoria now have designated areas.[4]

The *LCRA Act 2007* granted Victoria Police on-the-spot discretionary powers to ban individuals from a designated area for a period not exceeding 24 h (s148B(1,2)). This was increased to a maximum of 72 h under the *Justice Legislation Amendment (Victims of Crime Assistance and Other Matters) Act 2010* ('*JLA Act 2010*'). A police officer can impose a banning notice if he/she

(a) believes on reasonable grounds that the giving of the notice may be effective in preventing the person from—

  (i) continuing to commit the specified offence; or
  (ii) committing a further specified offence; and

(b) considers that the continuation of the commission of the specified offence or the commission of a further specified offence may involve or give rise to a risk of alcohol-related violence or disorder in the designated area [*LCRA Act 2007*, s148B(3)].

A banning notice may be imposed if a police officer reasonably believes that it may be effective in preventing the recipient from committing a specified offence or committing a further offence. Specified offences which are documented in the *LCRA Act 2007* (s7, schedule 2), include offences against the person, sexual offences, property damage, and assault.[5] However, it is not necessary for an offence to have been committed. A police officer is empowered to issue a banning notice in anticipation any perceived disorderly or anti-social behaviours. The legislation specifically references alcohol-related violence and disorder, but the behaviours for which banning notices may be imposed can reflect subjective perceptions and the interpretation of vaguely defined terms such as 'disorderly' and 'anti-social'. The *LCRA Act 2007* affords police officers the discretionary power to both define a behaviour as disorderly and to determine the punishment, by imposing a banning notice.

---

[3]In February 2012, the Director of Liquor Licensing was superseded by the Victorian Commission for Gambling and Liquor Regulation (VCGLR).

[4]The VCGLR website maintains an inventory of each designated area. The precise location for each is described and depicted visually on individual declarations (VCGLR 2017).

[5]Additional specified offences include trespass, offences relating to drunkenness, offensive and obscene behaviour, possession of prohibited weapons and failure to leave licensed premises.

Imposition of a banning notice requires that a police officer suspects "on reasonable grounds" (*LCRA Act 2007*, s148B(3)(a)) that an offence has been committed or is likely to be committed "wholly or partly in the designated area" (s148B(1)). The officer does not need to offer proof, demonstrate intent, or record any witness information. The banning notice sanction is imposed immediately and there is no possibility of legal representation. Police officers may also use "reasonable force" to ensure the banned person leaves the designated area (s148H).

Unlike other infringement provisions that permit the imposition of on-the-spot penalties, such as speeding fines,[6] there is no mechanism to seek an independent review of a police decision to issue a banning notice. Despite a range of recognised deficiencies across Victoria's infringement system,[7] recipients of other forms of infringement penalty may seek a formal review if they wish to challenge its imposition. Legal representation may be sought and evidence may be requested when a recipient instigates an appeal, and due process is therefore ensured prior to the punishment, typically a fine, taking effect. By contrast, the only avenue for a recipient of a banning notice to appeal its effect or validity, is by written notice to a police officer above the rank of sergeant, who may "vary or revoke a banning notice" (s148E). No appeal against the imposition of an individual banning notice is permitted beyond the agency of Victoria Police (Farmer 2017b).

In Queensland, the *Safe Night Out Legislation Amendment Act 2014* introduced police-imposed banning notices of up to ten days (s602C-D). The legislation expressly permits recipients to seek an independent review of the imposition of a ban via the Queensland Civil and Administrative Tribunal (s602P). Victoria's Civil and Administrative Tribunal (VCAT) does not have the remit to review police-imposed banning notice decisions.[8] There is no facility to appeal a police decision to impose an individual banning notice.

Although a banning notice is not a criminal sanction, its imposition is recorded on Victoria Police's Law Enforcement Assistance Programme (LEAP) database.[9] Breach proceedings may be initiated if a recipient is caught entering or attempting to enter the designated area (*LCRA Act 2007*, s148F). Banning notice breaches are strict liability offences. They operate under reverse onus principles, whereby the accused must prove the breach was a consequence of a mistake or was beyond their control (s148F(3a,b)). Breach penalties are initially financial, and are set at 20 penalty units

---

[6]For example, the *Infringements (Reporting and Prescribed Details and Forms) Regulations 2006* (Vic), r8, and the *Road Safety (General) Regulations 2009* (Vic), r75.

[7]Saunders et al. (2013) noted, for example, the disproportionate effect of fixed penalty fines upon less wealthy recipients.

[8]VCAT confirmed that "VCAT does not have jurisdiction to review this type of decision" [police-imposed banning notices] (personal email, 20 April 2015).

[9]Introduced in 1993, the LEAP database records Victoria's crime related data and information. It is used for operational policing and statistical analysis. Police officers and analysts record individual offences, penalties, missing persons etc. An individual's record may remain on LEAP indefinitely (Victoria Police 2012).

(currently $3171[10]). In the event of persistent non-compliance or non-payment of the fine, summary court proceedings may be initiated, with the potential for criminal consequences, including imprisonment (Farmer 2017b).

The way in which banning notices are framed has significant consequences for their imposition, and for the conception of balance. Banning notices are a quasi-criminal sanction, and embody a number of due process concerns. They may be imposed pre-emptively, take immediate effect, deny the recipient the opportunity to seek legal support, and provide no facility for independent appeal, despite potentially expansive breach provisions.

3.2 Research Methodology

Previous studies have used a mixed method approach to consider regulatory issues in the light of broader theoretical concepts, such as balance and punitiveness (Hall et al. 1978; Crawford and Lister 2007; Beckett and Herbert 2008, 2009, 2010a, b; Hadfield et al. 2009). This study draws on the success of the mixed method approach, and combines descriptive and exploratory methods to examine the rationale underpinning Victoria's banning provisions and to consider the consequences for the conception of balance.[11]

The research design applied multiple research techniques, including a contextual analysis of documentary sources, such as parliamentary records, Hansard, *Charter Act* guidelines and reviews, secondary analysis of published data, an examination of online media sources,[12] and interviews with a sample of Victorian Magistrates.[13] The research was conducted by a single researcher and comprised two key phases. The first phase analysed *Charter Act* documentation, Hansard records, and a range of additional secondary sources, to examine the rationale for Victoria's banning notice provisions. This informed consideration of how the need for banning was justified, and the extent to which the banning provisions were driven by what Crawford (2013) depicts as a desire to be seen to do something, regardless of both the 'need' and the effect upon individual rights and procedural protections.

---

[10]Penalty units are used throughout Victoria's legislation to quantify fine amounts (an offence may constitute a number of penalty units). Their value is set out and updated via Victoria's *Monetary Units Act 2004*. For the period 1 July 2017—30 June 2018, one penalty unit is $158.57.

[11]It does not seek to explain behavioural problems in Victoria's NTE or to evaluate the effectiveness of responses such as banning notices.

[12]Using *Newsbank*, an online News repository.

[13]The Magistrates' Court of Victoria (MCV) handles approximately 90% of all criminal and civil matters in the State. The remit of the MCV includes the determination of summary and some indictable offences, committal hearings for more serious indictable offences, and range of civil, family and specialist court functions (see: https://www.magistratescourt.vic.gov.au/about-us/about-court). Victoria does not follow the lay model of England and Wales. Magistrates in Victoria are fully qualified legal professionals.

The second phase combined published Victoria Police data (2008–2016) and media analyses ($n = 185$) with exploratory interviews with Magistrates ($n = 12$) to consider the ongoing scrutiny of the application of banning notices after their introduction. The data analysis applied straightforward descriptive methods to provide an overview of the use of banning notices in Victoria. No inferential analysis or tests of significance were conducted, as the published data did not facilitate this. The media analysis followed a simple search and coding method which is set out in Chapter Three. The decision to interview Magistrates reflects the research focus upon the potential due process implications of the banning notice provisions. As arbiters of procedural justice, it was decided to interview Magistrates to gain their perspectives. Following approval from the Chief Magistrate of Victoria, a written request was sent to every Co-ordinating Magistrate to seek willing interviewees. The sample was necessarily purposive, as it only included Magistrates. There are 51 Magistrates' Courts in Victoria, and all operate in the same way. Other than size, there is no discernible difference between the work undertaken in regional and metropolitan Magistrates' Courts. As the interviews were only one facet of the research, twelve were regarded as sufficient to gain an understanding of the perspective of Magistrates. The views expressed are not claimed to represent the views of the Victorian Magistracy as a whole. The interviews took place either in person or via Skype. Every interview was audio-recorded, and later transcribed verbatim. The second phase of the research addresses the contention that the legitimacy and broader consequences of discretionary police-imposed summary justice is essentially unknown, due largely to an absence of scrutiny. The key findings of the research are then drawn together to consider the appropriateness of 'balance' in the context of discretionary and pre-emptive police powers to punish.

The research applies a detailed contextual analysis of multiple document and data inputs. An inductive "immersion in data" (Hennink et al. 2011, p. 205) approach utilises both critical and interpretive analysis (Patton 1990). The analysis in relation to *Charter Act* compliance and the parliamentary debates is thematic and functional in purpose. It addresses the content and linear progress of the discourse and highlights key discursive structures (Van Dijk 1993; Chilton 2004). A body of sustained research has examined media reporting of crime and criminal justice policy.[14] The analysis of Newsbank records acknowledges the capacity of the media to shape policy (McCombs 2004; Altheide 2006; Beale 2006), and affect public perceptions of crime and justice (Gelb 2006). Newspapers are identified as one of the most influential contributors (Roberts and Indermaur 2009). Newsbank enables relevant media articles to be identified accurately, via key word search criteria.[15] The content of articles can then be analysed systematically (Riffe et al. 2005; Schreier 2012). Coding techniques produce meaningful data that can be assessed, compared, repeated or expanded as necessary (Krippendorff 2004). This study used preliminary assessment

[14]For example, Kidd-Hewitt (1995), Sacco (1995), Chibnall (2001), Lowry et al. (2003), Jones and Wolfe (2010), Silverman (2012), and Surette (2015).

[15]The analysis addresses the extent to which the articles enabled meaningful scrutiny of the banning notice provisions. Whether the media influenced the decision to introduce banning is not examined.

of relevant media articles to discern the categories. The resulting analysis required limited subjective interpretation, as it comprised a simple count and a determination of the primary purpose of each article.

Interview research enables a deep, focused and more personal understanding of issues. Interviews may take a number of general forms, from the fully scripted to the unstructured (May 2001). The semi-structured interviews used in this thesis draw together both extremes. Key themes are evident, and a level of comparability is enabled between interview findings. The specific direction of each interview may vary and provides a valuable tool for the discovery and examination of key themes (Jupp et al. 2000; May 2001). The interviews facilitate insight into the research issues from the participants' viewpoint; the insider or 'emic' perspective (Jupp et al. 2000; Hennink et al. 2011; Bartels and Richards 2011). The exploratory interviews with Magistrates examined experiences and perceptions of the banning notice provisions, and broader issues that they encompass.

The methodology and specific approaches used in this research combine to produce a contextual, in-depth, theoretically informed and internally valid examination of Victoria's banning notice provisions. It is emphasised that no evaluation of the effectiveness of banning notices has been undertaken. The accuracy of the documents and data collection is assumed and cannot be verified. The original reason for which documents and data have been compiled can limit both reliability and validity of subsequent analysis, as the content may reflect a pre-determined focus. However, the broader external assessment of the rationale upon which the banning legislation is based, and the extent of ongoing scrutiny of its application, informs analysis of the implications for the balance of individual rights and public protection in the administration of justice.

3.3 Rationale Underpinning Victoria's Banning Notice Provisions[16]

The arguments and rhetoric used to justify the passage of Victoria's banning notice provisions have been examined using an analysis of parliamentary scrutiny of the *Liquor Control Reform Amendment Act 2007* ('*LCRA Act*/Bill 2007') and the *Justice Legislation Amendment (Victims of Crime Assistance and Other Matters) Act 2010* ('*JLA Act*/Bill 2010'). Banning notices were presented to Victoria's Parliament as a straightforward response to alcohol-related disorder, and a sensible addition to the options available to police officers on the street. The provisions provided Victoria Police with a discretionary, pre-emptive power which limits personal freedoms and dilutes due process. There is no right to appeal against the imposition of a banning notice, but their breach may initiate penalties and criminal proceedings, which include fines and even imprisonment. The parliamentary debates of the two ban-

[16]The Analysis in This Section Expands upon and Synthesizes Findings Which Are Noted in Earlier Articles (Farmer 2014, 2016, 2017a, b).

ning bills reveal a number of underpinning assumptions and presumptions. Four key themes are set out here: a clear drive to 'do something' about alcohol-related disorder in the night-time economy (NTE); the promotion of fear and a consequential need to protect the broader community; an embedded notion of 'them' and 'us' in relation to banning; and a conflation of intent and punishment. In addition to the specifics of parliamentary discourse, the manner and extent of compliance with the *Charter Act* legislative processes highlights the deeper effect of such rhetoric, and is outlined in the final part of this section.

3.3.1 The Drive to 'Do Something'

Throughout the parliamentary debates of the LCRA Bill 2007 and JLA Bill 2010, across political perspectives, there was an assumption that a problem existed in Victoria's NTE that must to be addressed. Reflecting the general sentiment in 2007, Labor Assembly member Thomson summarised the concerns and the consequential need to do something.

> We also recognise that the levels of abuse around the inappropriate use of alcohol are increasing in and around some licensed venues, and we need to act on it. (Legislative Assembly 2007c, 4072)

Similarly, and representative of parliamentary concerns in 2010, Labor Council member Mikakos noted the same problems and associated need for a response.

> I support any measures that aim to reduce alcohol-fuelled violence and crime... it is important that these sorts of behaviours in public are not tolerated and that the police are armed with appropriate means to respond to them. (Legislative Council 2010, 1816)

The parliamentary discourse in both 2007 and 2010 was embedded with a presumed need for community protection against undesirable behaviours in the NTE, with the banning provisions presented as a necessary and appropriate response. That alcohol-fuelled disorder and anti-social behaviour occurs in the NTE is not disputed here. However, the extent of the problem, the way that it was conveyed across the parliamentary debates, and the effect this had upon establishing a hierarchy of rights implicit in the desired response, highlights concerns about the level of scrutiny in 2007 and 2010, and the priorities that resulted (Farmer 2016, 2017a).

Across the parliamentary debates of the LCRA Bill 2007, a number of speakers made reference to Victoria Police crime statistics or similar data regarding alcohol-related behaviours in the NTE to support the need for the banning provisions. For example, Liberal Assembly member O'Brien noted a 21.4% increase in assaults recorded in the Melbourne local government area [which includes the Melbourne Central Business District (CBD)] during the 2006–07 financial year (Legislative Assembly 2007b, 3998). Labor Council member Scheffer agreed and stated that during 2005–06 Victoria Police statistics recorded 29,000 assaults, "a significant number of which were contributed to by excessive alcohol consumption and occurred in and around licensed premises," and that there were "high numbers of offences in open spaces or areas near licensed premises" (Legislative Council 2007a, 3887). However, analysis of Victoria Police crime statistics suggests that the speakers applied convenient snapshot data, which lacked context and presented a misleading view of relevant crime rates (Victoria Police 2003, 2004, 2005, 2006, 2007). For example, the 21.4% increase in assaults noted by O'Brien included domestic assaults, which increased at a higher rate than the overall assault category between 2005–07, and which accounted for 36–37% of all assaults during this period. The statistics cited and alluded to in relation to assaults at licensed premises, by Scheffer, are similarly misleading. In the period 2003–06, Victoria Police crime statistics confirm that assaults at licensed premises decreased by 37%, from 2279 to 1429 per year. The claims of a significant number of assaults in licensed premises overlooks the prevailing downward trend. In the reporting year 2006–07, the figure for assaults in licensed premises did increase, by 7% to 1535. But this was still significantly lower than the numbers recorded in 2003 (2279) and 2004 (2144).

Scheffer's claim of high numbers of offences around licensed premises are also undermined by Victoria Police crime statistics for key offence categories that are relevant to the NTE, such as 'behaviour in public' and 'regulated public order' (Victoria Police 2005, 2006, 2007, 2008). The behaviour in public offences recorded on the 'street/footpath', which includes the areas around licensed premises, steadily decreased between 2005 and 2008, to a level below the 2001 figure. The number of such offences dropped by 19% in 2006 and a further 15% in 2007 (reducing from 2594 offences in 2005 to 1796 in 2007). Similarly, regulated public order offences taking place on the 'street/footpath' declined by 15% in 2006 and 10% in 2007 (from 1037 offences in 2005 to 793 in 2007). Both offence categories recorded at licensed premises do show some increase over the period. However, numbers are extremely low, and the trend was downwards during 2007. Across the whole State of Victoria, in 2005 only 140 behaviour in public offences were recorded at licensed premises. This figure increased to 147 in 2006 before reducing back to 114 in 2007. For regulated public order offences 149 were recorded at licensed premises across the whole of Victoria in 2005, 180 in 2006 and 178 in 2007. This data does not support the claim of "high numbers of offences" around licensed premises made to the Victorian Parliament by Scheffer.

In addition to a selective use of statistics, other speakers embedded their comments with assumptions that were not supported with any data or evidence. Nationals Assembly member Northe asserted that "the Bill will obviously address the rise of violence and assaults around licensed venues" (Legislative Assembly 2007c, 4070), but offered no specific data. Labor member Thomson observed "we also recognise that the levels of abuse around the inappropriate use of alcohol are increasing in and around some licensed venues" (Legislative Assembly 2007c, 4072). Nationals Council member Drum made a similarly assumption-based claim regarding "these increased trends of anti-social and violent behaviour" (Legislative Council 2007a, 3884). Such generalised claims were not evidence-based, and failed to quantify the nature of the problem in the NTE about which it was repeatedly asserted that something must be done. Significantly, no direct relationship was made between the problems articulated and banning notices as a solution.

The same problems of disorder in the NTE were claimed to support the need for the JLA Bill 2010. However, again, no evidence, quantification or data was presented in any of the debates in 2010 to justify extending the permissible length of banning notices. That a continuing need to address alcohol-related disorder in the NTE was perceived in 2010, despite the banning provisions being in place for over two years, itself questions the presumed effectiveness of banning notices. No evidence of the success or failure of banning as a mechanism to deal with such disorder was put forward during the debates in 2010. The Statement of Compatibility[17] noted only that "police have used the banning system effectively since its inception" (Legislative Assembly 2010a, 1132). Yet the efficacy and deterrent effect of banning, the Statement claimed, would be enhanced by extending the permissible length of a ban to 72 h. The success of banning as a mechanism to deal with disorder is not addressed explicitly here. However, the continued assertion that more needed to be done, two years after the *LCRA Act 2007*, suggests that banning may not have been as effective as expected.

3.3.2 Fear, Emotion and Community Protection

Analysis of the parliamentary debates of the LCRA Bill 2007 and JLA Bill 2010 reveals the use of legitimising and coercive strategies to build fear and to justify the proposed banning notice measures (Chilton 2004). The discourse emphasised the seriousness of alcohol-related problems in the NTE, which validated the legislative response to address the problem that had been presented. The drive to ensure community protection in the face of an immediate and tangible danger was repeated across all political perspectives in both 2007 and 2010. Liberal member O'Brien explicitly applied the language of fear during the 2007 debate, yet offered no credible evidence to validate his depiction of the issues he claimed faced the NTE.

> In a number of trouble spots throughout Victoria drunken hoons pose genuine threats to the property and physical safety of those who live nearby... the abuse of alcohol...[creates] a climate of fear for innocent people wishing to enjoy themselves responsibly. (Legislative Assembly 2007b, 3998)

Risks, both specific and general, were cited as an emotive vehicle to justify support for banning in the face of largely implied dangers. Typifying the technique, Labor Assembly member Thomson linked an assumption of violence and associated fear with the legislative response that would ensure community safety.

---

[17]The Statement of Compatibility ('the Statement') is tabled to both Houses of Parliament at the first reading of a Bill (Charter Act 2006, s28; Department of Justice 2008b, p. 27). Each part of a Bill which is considered to interact with a Charter right must be analysed in detail to confirm how the right is affected. A focused analysis of the Statements tabled for the banning notice Bills is set out in Farmer (2017a).

> We are not trying to be a wowser[18] state or trying to ensure that people cannot enjoy the occasional drink, but we want to ensure that people are safe and not fearful of abuse when they go to licensed premises; that is what this legislation is about - it is about minimising abuse in and around the consumption of alcohol. (Legislative Assembly 2007c, 4072)

Requests for an amendment permitting judicial appeal were countered by the Labor Minister Robinson with an entirely hypothetical response. Rather than offering evidence or research data, he used a fictional scenario to refute the need for an appeal process.

> You can just imagine it: you could have Alphonso[19] doing all sorts of antisocial things in Chapel Street. Under that earlier provision a police officer would come up and try to give him a banning notice. Alphonso would say, 'Hold on, I've got my lawyer here. I want you to withdraw the banning notice. We will see you in the Magistrates' Court tomorrow, and we will sort out the propriety of the banning order which is meant to apply now. We will sort that out in two or three weeks time' ... It would have been a lawyer's picnic. (Legislative Assembly 2007d, 4406 [Robinson, Labor])

The previous section noted some data and evidence that was used during the parliamentary debate of the LCRA Bill 2007 to support the concerns presented. In his assertion of "this plague" of alcohol-related violence creating a "climate of fear for innocent people" and a "battle" for the State, Liberal member O'Brien did cite Victoria Police crime statistics regarding rates of assaults (Legislative Assembly 2007b, 3998). However, the data was not specific to the NTE. Labor member Green presumed an increase in assaults inside licensed premises, but offered no actual figures (Legislative Assembly 2007b, 4007). Some attempt to quantify the perceived risk is acknowledged, but across the debates the provision of evidence was secondary to the presumed state of crisis. Layers of emotion were added to cement a sense of risk, using terms such as 'plague' and 'battle'. The legitimising and coercive strategies (Chilton 2004) asserted a moral authority to 'do something' with the corollary that any opposition was not moral.

Discursive structures were used to create a specific social representation (Van Dijk 1993). Basic emotions were invoked, including fear, security and protectiveness, particularly of family and the vulnerable. The discourse embodied approaches such as "fear systems", "emotion programs" and "kin-protection" (Hart et al. 2005, p. 191). In both 2007 and 2010, the case for banning was grounded in a moral position that was difficult to challenge. Labor Assembly member Green used parental concern for the safety of their children, and implied a clear physical risk.

> I, like every parent in this state, want my children to be able to enjoy Victoria's vibrant culture without having a concern that they may be hurt whilst enjoying that culture. (Legislative Assembly 2007b, 4007)

---

[18] A colloquial Australian term suggesting disapproval of alcohol.

[19] This is presumed to be a reference to prominent gangland figure Alphonse Gangitano, a noted frequenter of the NTE in Melbourne and later murdered as part of Victoria's gangland wars in the late 1990s and early 2000s. A controversial TV series was in well-publicised production at the time of these parliamentary debates.

Labor Assembly member Howard also specifically used concern about the safety of children to justify support for the LCRA Bill 2007. The term children implies vulnerability and dependence. It builds emotion and blurs the image of those who actually participate in the NTE. While they are all technically children, they are also mostly adults.

> Our community wants to know that our children are able to be out at night and to feel confident that they will come home safe and well, and this bill increases that sense of confidence. (Legislative Assembly 2007c, 4075)

Despite the rhetoric, anecdotes and hyperbole, objective analysis of the issues that banning notices are designed to address was not evident within the debates for either the 2007 or 2010 Bills. Justifications for banning were built upon implication and presumption, with limited use of data, much of which lacked context and specificity. In the light of *Charter Act* compliance requirements to empirically justify any limitation of Charter rights, and the extension of the banning provisions in 2010, the lack of objective information regarding the issues facing the NTE is problematic. The justification for the banning provisions reflected an all-embracing rationale of fear and a consequential need for community protection. The dominance of this discourse extended beyond the specific debate into the concrete provisions of the enacted legislation.

Advocates of the banning notice legislation emphasised the need to ensure community safety. Implied and assumed within this rhetoric is that banning works. The Statement of Compatibility for the 2007 Bill prioritised public protection against the problems caused by alcohol-related disorder.

> The Bill establishes two schemes directed at reducing alcohol-related violence or disorder. One enables immediate action to be taken by police officers, through the giving of notices banning persons from designated areas... [banning notices] are aimed at protecting public order and the rights and freedoms of others. (Legislative Assembly 2007a, 3818)

The 2007 Statement presumed the effect of banning notices, "to deter alcohol-related violence in and around licensed venues" (Legislative Assembly 2007a, 3822), but failed to provide any evidence to support either the nature of the problem or the suitability of banning as a response. The assumptions were not political party specific. Liberal member Napthine agreed with the presumed effectiveness of the banning notice provisions.

> These powers will ensure that we have an effective and workable response to the issues of alcohol and antisocial behaviour. (Legislative Assembly 2007c, 4070)

Labor member Foley succinctly stated the purpose of the banning notice provisions was "... to make our streets safer" (Legislative Assembly 2007c, 4077).

The same focus upon community safety was used to justify the extension of banning notices to 72 h in 2010. In the 2010 Statement of Compatibility, Attorney-General Hulls cited the *International Covenant on Civil and Political Rights (ICCPR)* which

> … expressly recognises that the right [to move freely] may be subject to restrictions that are necessary to protect public order, public health or morals or the rights and freedoms of others. (Legislative Assembly 2010a, 1131)

Hulls directly linked the presumed problems in the NTE, community protection and banning notices.

> The amendment is intended to increase the deterrent effect of banning notices, reduce the incidence of alcohol-related violence and disorder and, consequently, enhance public safety (1132).

However, Hulls did not provide any evidence to support the effectiveness of banning notices in protecting public order and the rights of others.

The assumption that banning works was deeply embedded in the parliamentary debate of the JLA Bill 2010 but no evidence was offered to support the requirement to extend the banning notice powers. There was only one exchange, in the Legislative Council on 6 May 2010, during which the use and effectiveness of banning was questioned. Greens member Pennicuik repeatedly requested evidence to justify the extension of the banning notice powers. Three times the Government response insisted that banning was working and making streets safer, but offered no proof of how this was determined or measured. That the same claims about the problems in the NTE were made in 2010 as in 2007, itself brings the effectiveness of banning into question. However, this paradox was not resolved in the parliamentary debates.

3.3.3 Notion of 'Them' and 'Us'

The parliamentary debates of the LCRA Bill 2007 and JLA Bill 2010 made clear that the overriding purpose of banning notices was to protect the community. The primacy of control and public safety was upheld, with banning "just a precautionary measure to allow police to control an area" (Legislative Assembly 2007c, 4072 [Thomson, Labor]). This perspective builds upon a persuasive discourse to legitimise a situation where the rights of individuals are conceded to the rights of the broader community. Implied is an assumption that the rights of those from whom the community needs to be protected are inherently lower. Both the 2007 and 2010 Statements of Compatibility referenced the rights of the community, despite the effect of the banning provisions upon the individual rights of recipients. The 2007 Statement noted that banning notices "are aimed at protecting public order and the rights and freedoms of others" (Legislative Assembly 2007a, 3818). The 2010 Statement similarly highlighted "the importance of protecting public order and the rights and freedoms of others" (Legislative Assembly 2010a, 1132).

This rhetoric subordinated the rights of individuals to the perceived needs of the community. This is a clear illustration of Waldron's (2003) 'few/most' balancing dichotomy, whereby addressing the needs of one side (the most) does not necessarily justify taking away the rights of the other (the few). The individuals most likely to be affected by the banning legislation were perceived differently to the community at large, and this embodied notions of them and us. Throughout the debates, parliamentarians presented themselves, their families and the majority of their constituents as the 'us' who deserved protection from the problem causing other, or 'them'. Alcohol-related problems in the NTE were expressly attributed to 'them', referred to variously as 'troublemakers', 'hoons', 'morons', 'thugs' and 'dingbats'. Liberal Assembly member O'Brien differentiated between them and us in his depiction of problems in the NTE.

> In a number of trouble spots throughout Victoria drunken hoons pose genuine threats to the property and physical safety of those who live nearby. (Legislative Assembly 2007c, 3998)

Labor Minister Robinson asked Liberal members if they "are going to continue to back thugs and criminals against decent, law-abiding Victorians" (Legislative Assembly 2007d, 4403), and emphasized the need to protect the good people against the behaviours of the bad.

> … to move some way towards the desired protections for those honest, law-abiding, decent Victorians against hooligans and the anti-social behaviour in nightclub precincts (4406).

'Troublemaker' was the term used most frequently across the parliamentary debates to describe those causing problems in the NTE. As a rhetorical device it highlighted those who behave in an undesirable way, but did not offer specificity or an objective assessment of behaviour which warrants the imposition of a discretionary on-the-spot penalty. Troublemaker is a widely understood term, but it is a vague, non-criminal label used to describe those for whom the quasi criminal banning notices were intended.

Examples have already been documented of scenarios and hypothetical situations whereby the problematic 'other' placed the needs, safety and rights of the predominant community in jeopardy. Labor Minister Batchelor epitomised the hyperbole.

> This is serious. You ask people who live near these venues and whose streets are affected by people who are drunk charging around the suburbs… (Legislative Assembly 2007d, 4405)

Batchelor's comment highlights the misleading and arguably manipulative nature of much of the rhetoric justifying the banning provision. The use of terms such 'suburb' and 'neighbourhood' suggest that alcohol-related violence is an imminent and serious risk in residential areas. Yet entertainment precincts and designated areas are not typically located in suburban residential districts. There is also an embedded assumption that the troublemaking 'other' do not reside in these 'suburbs,' further reinforcing the differentiation between 'them' and 'us'.

It is a reasonable expectation that the community should be free to enjoy themselves without fear or risk. How this freedom is effected creates a dichotomy, when it undermines the freedom and rights of individuals. The discourse evident across the parliamentary debates presupposed and reinforced a belief that banning notices are an essential response to issues in the NTE. The resulting limitations on individual rights were justified in the broader interests of the community. This brings into question the place of the affected individuals within that community (Waldron 2003). The undesirable minority become marginalised from both the process of debate and the consequences of the enacted legislation. In the case of banning notices, the arguments were built upon assumption-laden rhetoric by those who perceived themselves to be members of the 'us' group. The underlying attitude and response, with its resulting inequality and the silencing of the 'other', remained unchallenged. The parliamentary debates of the banning notice Bills embodied the paradoxical disjunction that we all have rights but some deserve more rights than others.

3.3.4 Conflation of Intent and Punishment

Victoria's banning notices dilute due process safeguards and weaken the separation of powers, through the coalescence of intent and punishment. The way in which the banning provisions were framed, and the limitations evident across their parliamentary scrutiny, conflates the notions of pre-emption, intent and punishment. Banning notices may be imposed following a discretionary assessment by a police officer of a potential future behaviour. The sanction carries a tangible limitation upon personal freedom, and an enduring record against a recipient's name. Implied throughout the banning legislation is the bundling up of more traditional responsive policing with anticipatory, pre-emptive controls and powers. Justifications which prioritised the interests of the greater good, and the need for public protection were used repeatedly across the parliamentary debates. The view was also presented across the discourse that, as banning notices are not criminal offences, they are not punishments.

The assertion that a banning notice is not a punishment is debatable. Banning notices are quasi-criminal in nature. They may be imposed as a consequence of an actual or potential behaviour, and place a measurable restriction upon recipients. Details of banning notices are also entered into Victoria's LEAP database, as an aid to enforcement, data tracking and the more complex consequences of multiple banning notice imposition. The impact and enduring electronic footprint of a banning notice is tangible, and there is no mechanism to remove it from an individual recipient's LEAP record. Significantly, breaching a banning notice, regardless of the basis of its original imposition, can lead recipients into the realms of criminal sanctions. Non-payment of initial financial penalties may lead to more far-reaching repercussions through established judicial processes. [20]

In supporting the LCRA Bill 2007, one Labor member stated "anybody... who is clearly out to cause violence... can be ordered not to re-enter for 24 h" (Legislative Assembly 2007c, 4075 [Howard, Labor]). How the intent to cause violence is to be assessed by police officers was not discussed and was not evident in any of the parliamentary debates. Assembly member Howard's layered rhetoric combined

[20]The ultimate sanction is imprisonment, in the event persistent non-compliance with the requirement to pay the penalty imposed. Under the *Infringements Act 2006*, "The Court may order that the infringement offender be imprisoned for a period of one day in respect of each penalty unit, or part of a penalty unit, to which the amount of the outstanding fines under the infringement warrant or warrants is an equivalent amount" (s160(1)). A banning notice breach may lead to a 20 penalty unit fine (see Footnote 10).

a reduction in the threshold for those targeted by the banning provisions, to include 'anybody', with a subjectively measured presumption of intent. Howard's comment raises the question of whether intent, however clear it may be, should be sufficient grounds for initiation of a police-imposed control. Once again, this perspective was absent from parliamentary debates in 2007 and 2010. Issues relating to the vagueness of the language and subjectivity of the interpretation of the behaviours to be controlled are noted earlier in this chapter. When added to the discretionary police power to determine intent, the resulting concerns increase further. A banning notice penalty may be based upon a subjectively measured presumption of intent. However, no evidence need be presented and the recipient has no opportunity to judicially challenge the validity of the on-the-spot decision by a police officer to impose a banning notice. Zedner (2007c) argues such conflations to be both morally and legally questionable. Neither imperative was adequately debated in 2007 or 2010.

In 2010, the JLA Bill extended the on-the spot banning notice to a maximum of 72 h. Attorney-General Hulls was unequivocal in his view that banning notices are not a punishment.

> ...the purpose of banning notices is not to punish persons for 'suspected' offences. Instead, they are designed to protect the community against alcohol-related violence and disorder, and to enhance the freedoms and rights of community members, such as the rights to life, privacy, liberty and security of the person and rights in respect of property. As such, I do not believe they should be regarded as punishment of a person, notwithstanding any deterrent effect they may have. Moreover, since banning notices per se do not amount to a person being charged with a criminal offence or being a party to a civil proceeding, they do not engage the Charter right to a fair hearing. (SARC 2010, pp. 14–15)

As their purpose is to protect, Hulls contended that banning notices should not be regarded as a punishment. In itself this is an interesting perspective on the notion of banishment and exclusion. Its specific relevance is highlighted when the precedent already set with respect to 24 h bans was used by Hulls to justify the extension of the banning period to 72 h, but with no supporting evidence despite over two years of operation. Hulls asserted that the potential impact of the increase to 72 h was not significantly or qualitatively different from that possible under the existing 24 h model. His formal response to SARC was sent after Royal Assent of the *JLA Act 2010*, therefore undermining the effectiveness of parliamentary scrutiny and accountability.

Hulls' assertions meant that someone could be excluded from a potentially large geographical area for 72 h, for an assumed pre-emptive reason, for which no evidence need be produced, but for which significant consequences may be invoked in the event of non-compliance. Hulls maintained that this scenario should not be regarded as a punishment or breach of human rights, as it had not been regarded as such before. That the period of banishment had been tripled was not deemed relevant by Hulls, as banning notices had already been approved on the overriding principle of protection of the public. Hulls' position justified the application of pre-emptive provisions which may carry prohibitive consequences, to support the basic right of the community to be safe (Finkelstein 2003; Oberdiek 2009). The contrasting perspective, summarised by Duff (2011), is that presumed intent and attendant pre-emptive prohibitions should only be used in the most serious circumstances. The extent to which the behaviours that may lead to a banning notice may pass this threshold is unclear, given the permitted subjective basis of their imposition. The potential consequences of the way in which the banning provisions are framed, particularly in terms of how much further such measures could be extended, were noted by only one speaker in the Legislative Council (Legislative Council 2010, 1813 [Pennicuik, Greens]). Her questions were not answered and her concerns were dismissed.

There was a notable absence of parliamentary scrutiny of Hulls' stated position that a banning notice is not a punishment.[21] There was also no meaningful consideration of any broader, longer term ramifications of the 2010 extension of Victoria's existing banning powers.

3.3.5 *Charter Act Compliance*

A key function of Victoria's bicameral parliamentary system is to pass legislation that is fair and proportionate (Parliament of Victoria n.d.). With the enactment of the *Charter Act*, a "new and common framework"[22] was introduced to support the development of statutory provisions, and to ensure that Bills are scrutinised to reflect the protections enshrined in the Charter. Both the LCRA Bill 2007 and JLA Bill 2010 were subject to the compliance requirements of the *Charter Act*, but the effect of the presumptions and assumptions which underpin the rationale for banning is evident in the way in which the *Charter Act* processes were applied.

Pre-enactment *Charter Act* compliance comprises three key stages, which are broadly sequential; initial policy analysis, impact assessment via a tabled Statement of Compatibility, and cross-party review by the Scrutiny of Acts and Regulations Committee (SARC), which is independent of analysis already undertaken. Initial policy analysis is typically classified as 'cabinet in confidence', and generally not available for public review.[23] The impact assessment for the Statement of Compatibility, therefore, builds on analysis that is not subject to open scrutiny, and feeds into the parliamentary debates. The SARC review typically runs concurrently with the parliamentary debates. The Statement of Compatibility ('the Statement') is tabled to both Houses of Parliament at the first reading of a Bill (*Charter Act 2006*, s28; Department of Justice 2008b, p. 27). Each part of a Bill which is considered to interact with a Charter right must be analysed in detail to confirm how the right is affected. If a Charter right is limited in any way by the proposed legislation, this limitation must be fully justified and any less restrictive means to achieve the same purpose must be considered (*Charter Act 2006*, s7(2)).

---

[21]This is explored further in the interviews with Victorian Magistrates, documented in Sect. 3.4.3.

[22]From the Victorian Government submission to the first four year Charter Review (Submission 324, cited in SARC 2011, p. 79).

[23]Unless a cabinet-in-confidence document is published during the term of a government it may not be released at a later date (SARC 2011, p. 79).

Rights are not absolute and may be waived where sufficient justification is evident. Section 7(2) of the *Charter Act* permits justifiable limitations upon the human rights it upholds. Any limitation of a Charter right must be "demonstrably justified". It is expected that research material and empirical evidence will be presented to support any proposed limitation, and must reflect "societal concerns that are pressing and substantial…more than just a common good must be strived for" (Department of Justice 2008b, p. 43).

An examination of the application of the *Charter Act* compliance procedures for the *Liquor Control Reform Amendment Act 2007* ('*LCRA Act 2007*')[24] and the *Justice Legislation Amendment (Victims of Crime Assistance and Other Matters) Act 2010* ('*JLA Act 2010*')[25] reveals notable omissions and questionable assumptions in relation to specific individual rights. Despite the clearly stated requirement, neither Statement of Compatibility ('2007 Statement' or '2010 Statement') included empirical evidence to justify even the acknowledged limitations of Charter rights, such as the right to move freely, the rights to privacy and reputation, liberty and security, and the presumption of innocence (as part of the rights in relation to criminal proceedings). The effect of the banning notices upon the right to a fair trial was missing from both Statements, and neither included any justification for the introduction of discretionary, police powers to ban. Banning notices were simply asserted to be necessary and effective. Despite the requirements of the *Charter Act 2006* (s7(2)), no alternative provisions were considered, and a general statement of the need to ensure public safety was the only explanation offered for the limitation of Charter rights.

The analysis undertaken as part of the SARC review of the Bills also failed to ensure effective consideration of the dilution of individual rights and due process protections. In both 2007 and 2010, SARC expressed concern about the effect of banning notices upon freedom of movement, liberty and the presumption of innocence, and the potential for key judicial principles to be undermined. However, these issues were not addressed effectively by the government. While SARC should ensure a meaningful cross-party scrutiny of legislative provisions, in the case of the banning Bills, the capacity of SARC to influence Charter compliance was largely ineffective.

Human rights are not necsssarily absolute, but Victoria's *Charter Act* is unambiguous in its expectation that policy and practice across government departments and public bodies must ensure than any limitations upon Charter protected rights are empirically justified (*Charter Act 2006*, s7(2); Golder and Williams 2007). The Charter Guidelines emphasise that government must "balance individual rights against each other as well as against other competing interests" (Department of Justice 2008b, p. 3). However, rather than balancing the provision of justice, failures in the expected scrutiny of the human rights implications of the banning notice provisions allowed the individual rights of recipients to be undermined. In this case, the formal human rights policy that is embodied in the *Charter Act* was not reflected in practice, and the consequences for individual rights of discretionary police-imposed banning notices were not subject to meaningful pre-enactment scrutiny.

---

[24] Which introduced 24 h police-imposed banning notices.

[25] Which extended the permissible length of a ban to 72 h.

It is useful to reflect on the meaning of both a reasonable limitation and its demonstrable justification. The term "reasonable" was used in the 2007 and 2010 Statements to substantiate each noted limitation upon a Charter right. What is meant by a 'reasonable' limitation is examined in the Charter's Guidelines (Department of Justice 2008b, pp. 42–47). Epitomising the balancing paradigm, the determination of reasonable limits is regarded as a "balancing exercise whereby the needs of the State are balanced against the rights of individuals" (p. 42). There is a clear expectation that

> the limit must impact the human right as little as is reasonably possible but still achieve the objective of the limitation as effectively. An excessive impairment will mean the limit is unlikely to be a reasonable one. (Department of Justice 2008b, p. 42)

The Guidelines make clear that the State is required to demonstrate that the reasonable limit is justified.

> … material should be available that demonstrates a limit is justifiable, such as studies, reviews, inquiries and consultation findings. Assumptions will not be enough (p. 42).

The *Charter Act* requirement for limitations to be based upon empirical evidence is not only to substantiate the need for any given right to be limited, but to support assertions of the effectiveness of the proposed limitation.[26] If the required evidence is not available, then it is difficult to justify a proposed limitation of a Charter right as being reasonable. The challenge of justifying new policy is acknowledged, particularly where no evidence of the success of a proposed new measure may yet exist. However, when the JLA Bill 2010 was introduced, the banning provisions had been operational for over two years. If sufficient evidence to support their need was available, it should have been presented in the 2010 Statement. That this key requirement of the *Charter Act* was not observed brings into question the rationale for the banning provisions, and certainly their extension to 72 h.

Despite clear expectations, no evidence, empirical or otherwise, was presented in support of any of the limitations outlined in either the 2007 or 2010 Statements. Issues of alcohol-related disorder in the NTE were claimed, and banning presented as a necessary and appropriate response. This absence of transparency created the potential for unseen political or other priorities to influence what should be a process of objective assessment. Lack of open disclosure of policy rationales or relevant research evidence enables legislative change to be built upon fundamentally flawed logic, which is opaque to meaningful pre-enactment scrutiny and challenge.

3.3.6 Summary

The parliamentary passage of both banning notice Bills demonstrate an unwavering determination to deal with the stated problem of alcohol-related disorder in the NTE.

---

[26]It is difficult to meaningfully evaluate the effect of a proposed new measure without a clear statement of its need and purpose.

Assertions of political necessity and community protection are used to justify compromises within the banning provisions that limit long standing due process rights, such as judicial appeal. Key consequences for individual rights and established procedural protections, resulting from the imposition or breach of a banning notice, were overlooked, denied or conceded to the interests of political expedience.

The failure of the *Charter Act* compliance process to justify empirically the dilution of individual rights that result from banning notices, in direct contravention of the *Charter Act*, was compounded by shortcomings in the evidence presented during the parliamentary debates to support the need for the provisions. Banning notices afford police officers the discretionary power to determine what an individual is likely to do, and to impose a pre-emptive penalty. Any assessment of the perceived intended behaviour is entirely subjective, and not open to independent scrutiny. Across the 2007 and 2010 parliamentary debates, descriptors and rhetorical devices ensured that the language applied to both the likely recipients of banning notices and those in need of protection was vague, but accessible and emotionally charged.

The picture painted in the parliamentary debates was of disorder in the NTE, embedded with an underlying notion of fear. Any political opposition to either the principle or specifics of banning was presented by proponents of the Bills as tantamount to supporting drunken disorder. Contributors to the debates, from both major political parties, emphasised problematic levels of alcohol-related issues from which protection was required. These presumptions underpinning the introduction of banning notices are not unique. They epitomise what Ashworth (2006) highlighted as symbolic responses to high profile issues about which a perception prevails that something must be done, regardless of the extent of the actual problem, and how appropriate or effective the response may be. The rationale upon which Victoria's banning notice Bills are based demonstrates a failure to heed the advice of Waldron (2003) and Zedner (2007a, b), that careful scrutiny of legislation is essential to ensure absolute clarity of the balance between the means and the ends.

3.4 Scrutiny of Victoria's Banning Notice Provisions

During the parliamentary debates of Victoria's banning notice Bills, a number of claims were put forward to substantiate the need for such provisions, and expectations were set regarding their ongoing scrutiny. The extent to which these claims and expectations have been revisited and re-assessed, have been explored through three key strands of post-enactment scrutiny. The first analysed nine years of formal Victoria Police banning notice data (2007–16), to consider the extent to which the published data has enabled meaningful scrutiny of the use of the discretionary police power to ban. The second strand explored media coverage of the banning notice provisions over the first five years of their use (2007–2012). The analysis examines how the legislation was addressed by the media, and considers whether this enabled purposeful public scrutiny of banning notices and their effect upon the individual rights of recipients. The final focus acknowledges judicial oversight and statutory interpretation as key tenets of the scrutiny and accountability of legislative provisions (Rares 2013). There has been no judicial review of the legality of Victoria's banning legislation or any aspect of its application, and there is no provision for independent appeal of individual notices. In the absence of any formal judicial consideration of the legitimacy of the banning legislation or the discretionary imposition of individual banning notices, interviews were conducted with a sample of Victorian Magistrates ($n = 12$). Their perspectives were sought on the due process and procedural implications of police-imposed banning notices, whether a right of appeal should be available, and potential broader consequences of the enactment of the banning notices powers.[27]

3.4.1 Published Banning Notice Data

During parliamentary debates of the LCRA Bill 2007, it was agreed that Victoria Police must publish annual banning notice statistics (Legislative Assembly 2007c, 4067–87; Legislative Council 2007a, 3861–899). This data was presented as a vehicle for the public scrutiny of the appropriate use of the banning provisions, the behaviours for which notices were imposed and, in particular, any disproportionate effect upon defined demographic groups. An amendment to trigger a review of the legislation if certain groups were found to be adversely affected was rejected in the Legislative Assembly (Legislative Assembly 2007d, 4401–4412).[28] The publication of recorded data was regarded as sufficient to ensure the correct use of banning notices. The *LCRA Act 2007* (s148R) stipulated that an Annual Report for each financial year[29] must be provided to Parliament by the Chief Commissioner of Victoria Police. Reports must include

- the number of banning notices imposed each year
- the number of people to whom orders have been given
- the number of multiple orders imposed each year (where a person has received more than one order)
- the "suspected specified offences in respect of which banning notices were given" (*LCRA Act 2007,* s148R(1)a(iv)) each year
- the designated areas where such offences were committed
- the ages of banning notice recipients
- indigenous status of banning notice recipients
- number of banning notices issued in each designated area
- number of charges in relation to breaches of banning orders, results of breach charges, and number of breaches for which no charges were laid (*LCRA Act 2007*, s148R).

[27]The research methodology and design is explained in Sect. 3.2.

[28]This related in particular to Indigenous and homeless Victorians.

[29]Ending 30 June.

Liberal Council member Lovell expressed a clear expectation that the published data would be used to facilitate public scrutiny of the way in which the banning provisions were applied by Victoria Police.

> ... any of the figures in the report indicating that particular groups are the subject of banning... orders should be the subject of public debate. (Legislative Council 2007a, 3894)

Compliance with the reporting requirements of the *LCRA Act 2007* (s148R), and the ongoing scrutiny of the published data has been assessed by analysing the Annual Reports covering the period 2007–16 (Chief Commissioner 2008, 2009, 2010, 2011, 2012, 2013, 2014, 2015, 2016).[30] No sampling was undertaken and no significance is inferred within or across a broader population. Data is published only at category level, such as age range or Indigenous status, rather than by individual banning notice. This constrained the complexity of the analysis as patterns were examinable only within each of the data categories. No cross-tabulation or other multi-variate analysis was possible. It was not known, for example, which age group received their bans in which designated area, or whether Indigenous recipients were more likely to receive a banning notice for a particular offence type. As it was not possible to report associations, relationships or correlations between or within the data, no tests of significance were required.

3.4.1.1 Trends in Banning Notice Imposition

During the first nine years of the operation of the *LCRA Act*, 6988 banning notices were issued. Figure 3.1 illustrates the number recorded in each of the Annual Reports, between 2008 and 2016. The trend initially rose, from 129 notices in the first (part) year, to a peak of 1868 in 2009–10. Numbers dropped significantly in 2010–11, reducing by more than half to 850 banning notices. Despite a small increase in 2011–12 the trend since 2012 has been sharply downwards, with only 143 banning notices recorded in the 2015–2016 reporting year. The reduction in the use of banning notices occurred during the same period that five new designated areas were declared.[31]

Table 3.1 documents the number of notices imposed in each designated area.[32] The figures suggest that the upward trend in 2011–12 may reflect continued growth in the number of designated areas, rather than an increase in the imposition of notices across each area. Most of the designated areas experienced a steady increase in banning notices imposed during the first two or three years of their designation. This was typically followed by a significant drop. There are exceptions to this general

[30]The Annual Reports include a summary of the data for the previous year. A number of minor differences are in evident in the data published in several of the Annual Reports. Where differences exist, the data published in the original report has been used in the analysis.

[31]Since the creation of the first two designated areas in December 2007, the number had increased to 20 by the end of June 2017.

[32]The designated areas are listed in the order in which they were declared.

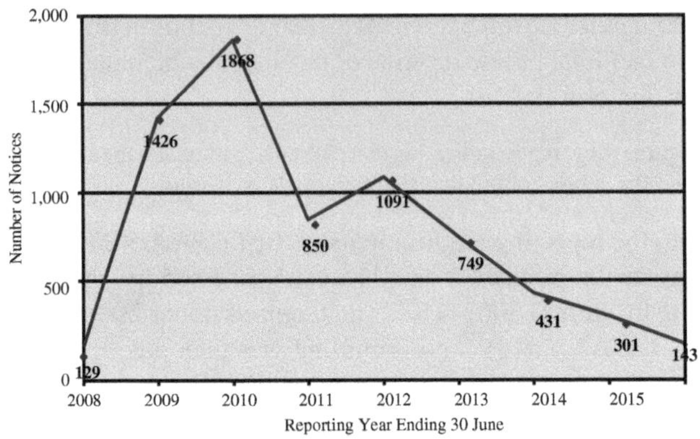

Fig. 3.1 Banning notices issued each year, 2008–16

trend. Prahran, Yarra, Frankston, Shepparton, Bendigo and Port Phillip/St Kilda all show initial growth, decline, and then growth again.

Of the 6988 banning notices imposed between 2008–2016, 5266 (75% of the total) were imposed in the Melbourne Central Business District (CBD). The next highest number, 318 (4.5% of the total) were recorded in Prahran, an inner Melbourne suburb. Across the remaining designated areas, the numbers of notices imposed each year was relatively low. That numbers were so low is an interesting finding. For example, despite being the second most populous city in Victoria, with over 140,000 inhabitants (ABS 2013), a maximum of 15 notices were imposed in Geelong in a whole year, and only 52 have been imposed over the nine year period. Given the justifications which must be put forward to secure designated area status,[33] and parliamentary claims of a behavioural crisis in the NTE necessitating the banning provisions, it is surprising that in some areas the banning notice powers have been used so sparingly. Knox, despite being designated in 2008, has imposed only one banning notice over the whole nine year period.

The use of banning notices has fluctuated, over time and place, but the data confirms that they are used. Trends that are evident in the data can only be examined at a high level, which limits the analysis that is possible. In particular, as the dates on which banning notices were imposed are not reported, the published data does not enable sufficient analysis to link imposition patterns with particular operational enforcement initiatives or 'hot spot' activities.[34] Nevertheless, with 6988 issued during the first nine years, banning notices have been used widely. This elevates debate and concern about their potential effect to be more than just conceptual or theoreti-

[33]These are outlined in Sect. 3.4.1.4.

[34]Precise reasons for the fluctuating use of banning notices are outside of the scope of this book. Explanations may include changes in operational and policy priorities, an expansion in the options available to police officers, such as move-on powers and an increasing range of infringement provisions, and the possible success of banning notices in changing the behaviours of recipients.

Table 3.1 Number of banning notices each year by designated area

Area	Start date	2008	2009	2010	2011	2012	2013	2014	2015	2016	Total
Melbourne	*Dec 2007*	121	1197	1639	681	667	435	288	151	87	**5266**
Prahran	*Dec 2007*	8	88	53	18	88	41	17	5	0	**318**
Ballarat	*Aug 2008*	–	18	60	64	14	5	5	2	0	**168**
Geelong	*Aug 2008*	–	15	5	15	6	3	3	5	0	**52**
Port Phillip/St. Kilda	*Aug 2008*	–	22	13	14	28	89	21	12	1	**200**
Warrnambool	*Aug 2008*	–	9	1	17	3	0	1	8	0	**39**
Yarra	*Aug 2008*	–	10	24	7	1	11	1	2	2	**58**
Bendigo	*Sep 2008*	–	20	32	8	0	45	5	1	1	**112**
Knox	*Sep 2008*	–	0	0	0	0	0	1	0	0	**1**

(continued)

Table 3.1 (continued)

Area	Start date	2008	2009	2010	2011	2012	2013	2014	2015	2016	**Total**
LaTrobe/Traralgon	*Oct 2008*	–	45	21	5	8	11	9	15	3	**117**
Frankston	*Mar 2009*	–	2	11	6	25	20	3	6	1	**74**
Shepparton	*Mar 2010*	–	–	9	15	14	5	8	21	19	**91**
Dandenong	*Apr 2011*	–	–	–	0	214	41	5	0	1	**261**
Docklands	*May 2011*	–	–	–	0	23	6	3	2	0	**34**
Mildura	*May 2012*						23	38	29	17	**107**
Footscray	*Aug 2012*						4	12	2	0	**18**
Colac	*June 2013*							1	2	1	**4**
Mornington	*May 2013*							3	31	8	**42**
Sunshine	*Sep 2015*									0	**0**
Unclassified							10	7	7	2	**26**
Total		**129**	**1426**	**1868**	**850**	**1091**	**749**	**431**	**301**	**143**	**6988**

cal, and justifies an exploration of the broader consequences for due process and the erosion of individual rights.

3.4.1.2 Vulnerable Recipients of Banning Notices

Prior to the implementation of the LCRA Bill 2007, Greens Party Council Member Hartland expressed concern about the potential effect of banning provisions on disadvantaged groups, in which she specifically included homeless and Indigenous persons (Legislative Council 2007a, 3882). It is not possible to discern from the published data how many recipients of banning notices were homeless. Despite the inclusion of *'no fixed place of abode'* as an option on the banning notice form, this detail is not recorded centrally. The effect of the discretionary police power to ban upon the homeless is therefore unknown. It is also not known how many other vulnerable recipients, such as people with mental health issues, have been affected or how appropriately the banning provisions have been used.

The *LCRA Act 2007* did set a clear expectation that data will be reported regarding the Indigenous status of recipients of banning notices: "whether any of the persons to whom banning notices were given during that year were of Koori[35] origin" (*LCRA Act 2007,* s148R(1,a,vii)).[36] The published data recording the Indigenous status of banning notice recipients is summarised in Table 3.2.

Three Indigenous status categories are included in the published banning notice data: Indigenous,[37] non-Indigenous or unknown.[38] The percentage of banning notices given to recipients recorded as being Indigenous fluctuated between 2% and 5% over the nine years analysed, with an average of 3.2% of the total number each year. This is notably higher than the Indigenous percentage of the resident population of Victoria. Australian Bureau of Statistics (ABS) data sets the figure at 0.6% in 2006, rising slightly to 0.7% in 2011 (ABS 2006, 2011). While the actual numbers of banning notices given to Indigenous recipients may be low, it is clear that the relative percentage when compared with the resident population of Victoria is disproportionately high.

[35] Koori refers to people of Indigenous descent in Victoria and parts of New South Wales.

[36] This requirement reflects longstanding concerns about racially discriminatory policing practices. Research into US, UK and Australian policing has explored the way in which discretionary police powers, such as to move-on and stop/search, have been used disproportionately against certain racial groups. For example, Weitzer and Tuch (2002), Weatherspoon (2004), Tyler and Wakslak (2004), Goodey (2006), Hallsworth (2006), Harris (2006), Walsh and Taylor (2007), Sivasubramaniam and Goodman-Delahunty (2008), Young (2010), Grossman et al. (2013), Yesufu (2013), and Mazerolle et al. (2013).

[37] The banning notice form includes the options 'Aboriginal', 'Torres Strait Islander' or 'Both' to describe the origin of Indigenous recipients. These are conflated into the reporting category 'Indigenous.'

[38] The published data includes two line items: 'unknown' and 'unspecified.' These have been conflated for the purposes of this analysis as they both reflect an 'unknown' Indigenous status.

Table 3.2 Banning notices issued per year, by Indigenous and non-Indigenous recipients; % of total (and actual numbers) each year

Year ending	Total bans	Indigenous % (actual)	Non-indigenous % (actual)	Unknown % (actual)
30 June 2008	129	5% (7)	94% (121)	0
30 June 2009	1426	3% (40)	83% (1182)	14% (204)
30 June 2010	1868	3% (60)	82% (1535)	15% (273)
30June 2011	850	3% (29)	50% (427)	46% (394)
30 June 2012	1091	3% (31)	62% (681)	35% (379)
30 June 2013	749	4% (29)	50% (371)	47% (349)
30 June 2014	431	4.5% (19)	39% (168)	57% (244)
30 June 2015	301	3% (9)	33% (100)	64% (192)
30 June 2016	143	2% (3)	38% (54)	60% (86)
	6988	**3.2% (227)**	**66.4% (4639)**	**30.4% (2121)**

Due to rounding, percentages may not add up to 100% (The actual numbers for 2008 do not add up to the total. There was one instance of a multiple banning notice, whose recipient is only recorded once in these figures. Subsequent reports include the relevant data for each notice issued.)

Across the nine year period studied, there were marked changes in the relative percentages for each of the Indigenous status categories, depicted in Fig. 3.2.

In contrast to the relatively stable proportion recorded as Indigenous, the percentage of banning notices given to recipients of non-Indigenous status declined notably. The figure dropped from 94% in the first reporting year, to 33% in 2014–15, and averaged 66.4% over the nine years analysed. When added to the disproportionate number of bans imposed upon Indigenous recipients as a whole, a significant issue is evident. The risk of adverse consequences for specific groups was noted during parliamentary debates of the banning provisions in 2007. The published data was offered as a mechanism to monitor this. However, despite the issues that are identifiable in the data, neither the legislation or the manner of its implementation have been re-visited. The effect of banning notices upon the Indigenous population of Victoria has been subject to no public or subsequent parliamentary scrutiny.

The reliability of the published data is further affected by a lack of clarity about how the Indigenous status of banning notice recipients has been determined. The first Annual Report publishing banning notice data articulated the process to be followed.

> Koori identification status was based upon the existence of at least one instance of self identification recorded against the person. (i.e. an answer of either Aboriginal, Torres Strait Islander, or Both Aboriginal and Torres Strait Islander to the question: are you of Aboriginal and/or Torres Strait Islander origin?) (Chief Commissioner 2008).

However, subsequent Annual Reports did not contain this procedural note. It is not known whether the classifications noted in the published data were derived by recipient self-report or from assumptions made by issuing police officers. Patterns in the data are indicative of either a failure to ask, or an increasing use of assumption-

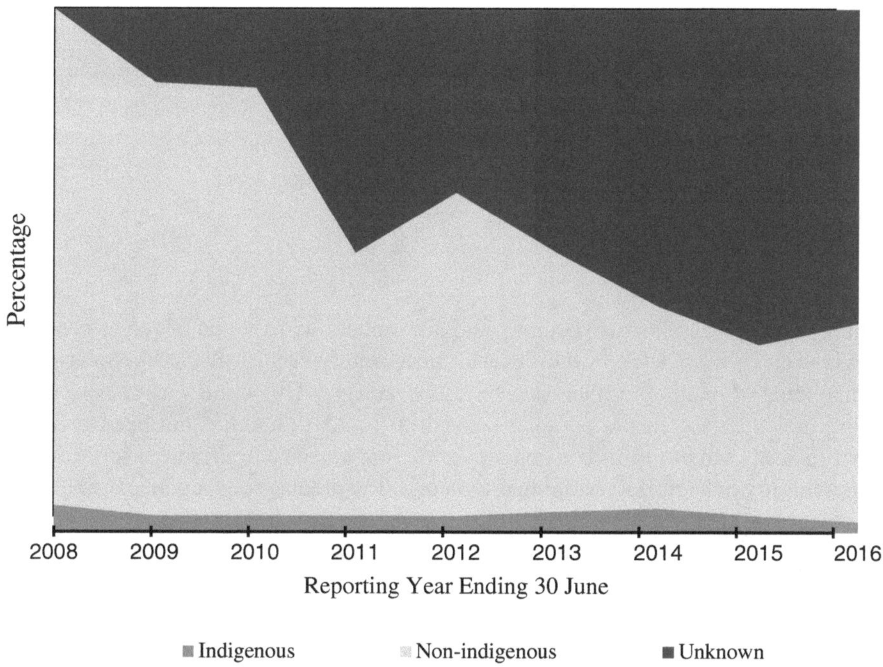

Fig. 3.2 Indigenous status of banning notice recipients, as % of total issued each year

based categorisation, similar to the subjective assessment of racial appearance from which the Victoria Police Crime Statistics data is derived (Victoria Police 2008, p. 7). This is most apparent in the steady increase in the number of banning notice recipients whose Indigenous status was recorded as unknown, which rose from 14% of the total in 2008–09 to a peak of 64% in 2014–15, and averaged 30.4% over the nine years. Failure to ask, observation and assumption are the most likely sources of an 'unknown' assessment. This not only creates clear potential for error if simple visual appearance is the basis of the categorisation, the use of 'unknown' or 'unspecified' enables the disproportionate use of banning notices for Indigenous Victorians to be hidden in the data. In the first annual report (2007–08), in which the 'unknown' and 'unspecified' categories were not used, 5% of banning notice recipients were recorded as Indigenous: more than eight times higher than the Indigenous percentage of the Victorian population in 2006 [which was 0.6% (ABS 2006)].

The lack of accurate data regarding the Indigenous status of banning notice recipients is a notable issue. Despite the expectations of accountability, reflected in the *LCRA Act 2007* requirement to publish banning notice data, the actual proportion of banning notice recipients who are of Indigenous origin is simply not known. As a result, public examination and scrutiny of the operation of the legislation, and the particular effect of the discretionary police power to ban upon the Indigenous population, appears to be compromised. In the context of a body of research into discriminatory

Table 3.3 Multiple banning notices issued each reporting year, 2008–16

	2008	2009	2010	2011	2012	2013	2014	2015	2016
Number of unique banning notice recipients	128	1384	1803	831	1005	709	394	287	125
Number of multiple notices issued	1	33	54	19	86	18	17	7	9

policing of Indigenous Australians[39] and subsequent admissions of racial profiling by Victoria Police (2013),[40] the failure to accurately record the Indigenous status of recipients of banning notices is a serious oversight. This issue was not discussed during the extension of the banning provisions in 2010, and has not been revisited in parliament, which reinforces concern about the absence of effective scrutiny and accountability of Victoria's banning provisions. The precise consequences of banning for vulnerable recipients, such as Indigenous Victorians and the homeless, remains unknown.

3.4.1.3 Multiple Banning Notice Recipients

In the Statement of Compatibility for the JLA Bill 2010, Attorney-General Hulls linked the issuing of multiple bans with justifications for extending the permissible length of individual banning notices to 72 h.

> … there have been a number of people to whom police have had to give a banning notice on multiple occasions… its efficacy can be enhanced through enabling police, in appropriate circumstances, to give notices of a significantly longer duration. (Legislative Assembly 2010a, 1132)

Table 3.3 documents the number of multiple (more than one) bans imposed during the first nine years of the operation of the banning provisions.

In the first two years, for which data had been published when the 2010 Statement was tabled by Hulls, banning notices were given to 1512 individuals, of whom 34 (or 2.2%) received more than one notice (Chief Commissioner 2008, 2009).[41] While

[39]For example, Johnston (1991), Luke and Cunneen (1995), Cunneen (2001), Paradies (2005), Walsh and Taylor (2006, 2007), and Crofts and Mitchell (2011).

[40]A report by Victoria Police in 2013 admitted racial profiling by police officers. This case did not relate to the profiling of Indigenous Victorians, but it highlighted racially discriminatory practices within Victoria Police. In 2010, six Australian men pursued a civil case in Melbourne's Federal Court, claiming racial discrimination in Flemington and North Melbourne between 2005 and 2009. The case was settled out of court by Victoria Police. As part of the settlement, admissions were made. A full inquiry into public relations and training was conducted (Grossman et al. 2013; Victoria Police 2013).

[41]The published data for the first two reporting periods only specified the number of multiple notices. Later reports included a breakdown for individuals receiving 2, 3, 4 and more than five notices.

supporting Hulls' claims of multiple order impositions, the actual number issued was low. The figures are not indicative of a need to extend the duration of banning notices to prevent their multiple imposition. This data was available to be scrutinised but was not referenced during the 2010 parliamentary debates. By contrast, of the 5154 individual banning notice recipients recorded between years ending 30 June 2010 and 30 June 2016, 210 (or 4.1%) received more than one order. While still a low absolute number, the percentage of multiple order recipients had nearly doubled from 2.2% over the first two reporting periods (2007–08 and 2008–09).

If extending the permissible length of a ban was an effective deterrent, as claimed by Hulls, the proportion of multiple order recipients should not have increased. The enhanced effect of longer banning notices, used to justify their extension to 72 h, does not appear to be evident. Yet there has been no subsequent parliamentary or public consideration of the use of 72 h banning notices or their effectiveness when compared with 24 h bans. Furthermore, the data does not record the length of each banning notice imposed, so there is no way to scrutinise compliance with the 'in appropriate circumstances' requirement for the imposition of 72 h bans.

3.4.1.4 Designated Areas

A pre-requisite for the imposition of banning notices is the designation of declared areas in which they will apply. The steady increase in the number of designated areas that has occurred since 2007 (documented in Table 3.1), reflects a clear assumption that banning notices are a necessary provision to address issues relating to alcohol consumption in the NTE. However, the threshold for the declaration of a designated area is fluid and not objectively defined. No guidelines are evident in the banning notice legislation, parliamentary debates or subsequent Victorian Commission for Gambling and Liquor Regulation (VCGLR) documentation relating to designated areas. There are no firm or measurable rules that must be applied before a district can be declared a designated area, beyond the legislated requirement that the VCGLR "believes" that alcohol-related violence and/or disorder has occurred in the vicinity of licensed premises within a particular area, and that a designated area will be an effective response (*LCRA Act 2007*, s147(1)). Data and reasons in support of designation are presented to the VCGLR by affected stakeholders, such as Victoria Police and local councils. The cases put forward for designation are not typically publicly available and how the VCGLR effects its decision remains unclear.[42]

The declaration of designated areas presumes the effectiveness of banning notices in controlling alcohol-related disorder in the NTE. In four of the first five Annual Reports the reasons for the imposition of banning notices were not published. As a result, meaningful cross-tabulation with Victoria Police Crime Statistics is limited

[42]This study has not tested the rationale for each designated area declaration. However, it is noted that parliamentary justifications to designate the Melbourne CBD and Chapel Street/Prahran areas in 2007 were largely anecdotal, or supported with vague or selectively applied crime data. It is not known if further evidence was presented to the then Director of Liquor Licensing prior to their declaration.

and any causal linkage is difficult to substantiate. It is not known, for example, how many of the 1639 banning notices issued in the Melbourne CBD in 2009–10 were for reasons of alcohol-related violence and how many were a subjectively assessed pre-emptive police response to a potential nuisance. The difference is significant when seeking to understand and scrutinise the application of the discretionary police power to ban, the parliamentary justifications for which focused upon what were presented as tangible issues of alcohol-related disorder.

Statements accompanying the declaration of designated areas typically make reference to generic concerns. A government media release following the declaration of Dandenong (in Outer Eastern Melbourne), explained that the designation was "at the request of local police concerned with violence and anti-social behaviour in the area" (O'Brien 2011a). Similarly, the media release that accompanied the declaration of Melbourne's Docklands stated

> The ability to issue banning notices within Docklands will give police the power to act quickly to prevent anti-social behaviour before it happens... These measures will deliver improved safety for the precinct's growing number of residents, workers and visitors and help licensees better manage their venues. (O'Brien 2011b)

However, other than in the first part-Annual Report (published in 2008), no data was included which noted the offences for which banning notices were imposed until the 2012–13 Annual Report. This hinders analysis of the way in which the banning provisions were used. In addition to the gaps identified in the early iterations of published data, there appears to be an incompatibility between the needs that are claimed prior to designation and the operational policing experience. Designated areas have been declared to cover the key entertainment precincts and hubs within Victoria's main towns and cities. The low number of banning notices issued in some designated areas has already been noted. In Knox, only one ban has been imposed in the nine years since designation in September 2008. Given the arguments that must be put forward to secure designated area status, it is surprising that the discretionary power to ban has not been used more widely. However, the designated area status for Knox has not been reviewed since its declaration. Later designated area declarations are set for periods of 12 months—and are subject to an annual renewal. How this process works remains unclear. The Colac CBD, for example, has received three designated area renewals, despite imposing only four banning notices since its initial declaration in June 2013—bringing into question the need for the Colac CBD to be a designated area as an 'effective response' to issues in the NTE.[43]

Designated area declarations place great emphasis upon crime prevention in the interests of public safety, and are often emotive, vague and couched in terms to generate fear. In announcing Dandenong a designated area, the Minister for Consumer Affairs hailed the extension of "new laws to deal with drunken, loutish and threatening behaviour" (O'Brien 2011a). Banning provisions were presented as a proactive mechanism to ensure community safety, "... rather than wait for something to happen, banning notices can be used to defuse situations and remove troublemakers

[43] It is possible that the general deterrent effect of banning accounts for the low number of notices issued in some designated areas. However, there is no empirical evidence to support this.

from harmful situations" (O'Brien 2011a). The 2011 designated area declaration in Docklands continued the rhetoric: "... people doing the right thing should be able to enjoy the sport and nightlife on offer in the Docklands without their fun being spoiled by a few louts" (O'Brien 2011b). However, public scrutiny of the way in which the discretionary police power to ban is being used is limited. The claims made to justify the designation of new areas cannot be tested, and are not publicly examinable.

3.4.1.5 Summary

The way in which banning notice data has been published limits meaningful scrutiny of the banning notice provisions and of the need to 're-balance' the provision of justice in the NTE, that is implicit in both the legislation and the declaration of designated areas. The lack of detail in the published data inhibits meaningful and comparative analysis of the use of banning. Ongoing assessment of how banning notices are being used would be informed by the inclusion of measurable baselines and points of comparison, such as dates, times, specific locations and behaviours.

The publication of data relating to the imposition of banning notices was a clearly stated requirement of the *LCRA Act 2007* (s148R), regarded as essential to facilitate public scrutiny and to ensure that no specific demographic group is affected disproportionately. The way in which the data has been published, in particular the uncertainty about the Indigenous status of recipients and the lack of offence specific data in the first five reports, raises fundamental concerns. Effective public scrutiny of the use of the discretionary police power to ban is both necessary and a legislative requirement. The banning provisions have been justified in parliament and within designated area applications as essential to 're-balance' community protection in the NTE. However, the data that should enable objective examination of their use falls short of mandated expectations. Significantly, despite the banning notice data being formally tabled each year, the findings and deficiencies noted in this analysis have not been explored by Victoria's Parliament.

3.4.2 Media Scrutiny

The media can be instrumental in constructing a social agenda which directs and reinforces the need for legislative change (Hall et al. 1978; McCombs 2004; Altheide 2006; Beale 2006; DCPC[44] 2001, 2010; Jones and Wolfe 2010; Silverman 2012). The depiction of issues in the media influences both public perception of crime and criminal justice policy. Media coverage can also serve as a check upon decisions made by policy makers, policing behaviours, and criminal justice processes (Surette 2015). The media remains a key influence upon public perceptions and a primary source of public scrutiny (Gelb 2006; Roberts and Indermaur 2009). A "robust media" (AHRC

---

[44] Victorian Parliament Drugs and Crime Prevention Committee.

Table 3.4 Total banning notice specific articles, 2007–12

Year[a]	Total articles
2007	23
2008	73
2009	49
2010	18
2011	20
2012	2
Total	**185**

[a]Calendar year

2009, p. 2) should act as an essential check on government powers by ensuring public awareness of key issues. To extend the examination of the scrutiny of Victoria's banning provisions, an analysis of the media coverage of their implementation considered whether the use of the new police powers, or their consequences for due process procedural protections and individual rights, were subject to media-driven public scrutiny.

The research examined coverage of banning notices in Victorian newspapers ($n = 55$) that were accessible via the online repository Newsbank.[45] Fifty of the titles are local publications, and five have a state-wide circulation. An 'any text' key word search was undertaken for the period 2007–12.[46] Each article retrieved was accepted for analysis only if it specifically referenced the banning notice provisions relevant to this study.[47]

3.4.2.1 Number and Source of Articles

The number of individual articles that specifically referenced the banning notice provisions was 185. Table 3.4 documents the total number returned for each year. Most of the relevant media articles were published in 2008 and 2009 (122, or 66% of the sample), directly after the banning provisions were first introduced.

[45]Additional print media sources exist beyond those utilised by Newsbank, in addition to a wealth of online media. Newsbank is sufficiently representative to reveal trends and detail in the coverage.

[46]This enabled examination of the media coverage of the first five years of the provisions. The data is documented by calendar year.

[47]The initial search returned 6413 articles. Due to the broad search terms used, the majority of the articles retrieved related to other types of banning that were prominent in the media. Examples include sunbeds, smoking, smacking, puppy farms, live cattle exports, fracking and using mobile phones while driving. These articles were excluded from the analysis.

Table 3.5 Media content analysis categories and identifiers

Core focus	Description	Identifier
Imposition of the legislation and/or a specific relevant strategy	Primary focus upon the imposition (potential or actual) of the banning notice legislation. Including reporting the declaration of designated areas, and how the provisions relate specifically to strategic plans addressing issues in the NTE	**Imposition**
Specific events	Reporting details of particular dates, events, initiatives or police operations in relation to the NTE, and in which the banning provisions are referenced	**Event**
General concern	Documenting general concern about behaviour in the NTE, including discussion of the banning provisions. Generally more editorial expressions of concern regarding the NTE and banning provisions	**Concern**
Data	Primarily reporting published data relating to the banning provisions	**Data**
Judicial concern/Legal challenge	Relating to judicial (rather than political or personal) discussion of banning issues, and specific court cases or legal challenges	**Legal**

3.4.2.2 Primary Purpose of Articles

The content of each relevant article was analysed to discern its primary purpose. Five categories were established against which to capture the core focus. Each is defined in Table 3.5, along with the identifier used in the subsequent analysis. If an article could fit into more than one category its primary purpose was determined. For example, an article that focused upon concerns about behaviours in the NTE, but which included a reference to banning notice data within a particular area or timeframe, was categorised under '*Concern*'. This decision was made subjectively by a single researcher following a reading of each article. The results of the detailed analyses of each article are contained in Table 3.6.

The most common article focus over the six year period related to the '*Imposition*' of the banning legislation, comprising 112 (or 61%) of the 185 articles. This coverage was at its peak in the immediate aftermath of the enactment of the *LCRA Act 2007*, and tended to reflect the surge in designated area declaration (noted in Table 3.1), and associated reporting in local newspapers. For example, prior to the designation of Geelong in 2008, the local paper (*The Geelong Advertiser*) ran a series of articles in April, May and June highlighting plans to introduce banning. Five more articles were published in August, following the declaration of Geelong as a designated area

Table 3.6 Primary purpose of banning specific articles, 2007–12

Year	Imposition	Event	Concern	Data	Legal	Total
2007	17	2	3	1	0	**23**
2008	57	2	7	7	0	**73**
2009	20	3	13	11	2	**49**
2010	5	0	2	11	0	**18**
2011	13	0	2	3	2	**20**
2012	0	2	0	0	0	**2**
Total	**112 (61%)**	**9 (5%)**	**27 (15%)**	**33 (18%)**	**4 (2%)**	**185 (100%)**

Percentages are subject to rounding

Across all publications, the articles in the '*Imposition*' category primarily reported the declaration of new designated areas and the use of banning notices as a generally welcomed mechanism to address issues in the NTE. Example headlines included:

> Bans on drunks, thugs to spread (*Sunday Herald Sun*, 20 April 2008)
>
> Drunks face ban. Police target late-night hotspots
>
> (*Port Philip Leader*, 11 August 2008)
>
> Police welcome Knox O-zone ban powers
>
> (*Knox Leader*, 30 September 2008)

The irony of the headline in the *Knox Leader* is noted, as the analysis of published banning notice data revealed that no bans were imposed in Knox between 2008 and 2012.

Published banning notice '*Data*' was the focus of 33 (18%) of the 185 articles. However, each article limited the reporting of the data to straightforward numbers of notices imposed. There was no analysis or discussion of the data in any of the 33 articles. For example, there was no consideration of issues relating to the effect of banning notices upon Indigenous Victorians, or of any limitations in the published data. Despite the expectations expressed during parliamentary debates of the LCRA Bill 2007, the published data was not a vehicle for the public scrutiny of the imposition and consequences of the banning provisions.

Of the 27 articles (15%) that discussed general '*Concern*' in relation to the NTE and alcohol-related behaviours, and which specifically referenced banning notices, there was no consideration of any issues relating to the banning provisions themselves. Banning notices were regarded as a proactive tool to target the causes of the general concern. For example, the Chief Commissioner of Victoria Police, Simon Overland, wrote in the *Herald Sun* in 2011.

> New laws have complemented a more visible and active presence. We ban troublemakers from licensed precincts... The evidence suggests that these and other initiatives are starting to work... (*Herald Sun*, 15 February 2011)

All of the articles addressing general '*Concern*' about alcohol-related issues in the NTE extended the parliamentary assumption that banning notices were a necessary and appropriate response, without offering supporting evidence.

Only nine articles across the six year period focused primarily upon '*Events*' and operational activities. For example, following the passage of the *LCRA Act 2007*, *The Geelong Advertiser* reported that "Police will conduct a crackdown on licensed premises across Victoria this summer" (19 December 2007). Once again the article contained an underlying rationale that a problem existed in the NTE that must be addressed, and provided no challenge to or analysis of the provisions.

Across the six year period between 2007 and 12, only four articles addressed '*Legal*' considerations or judicial concerns related to the banning provisions. Two referenced banning in passing in the context of legal powers to manage issues in the NTE (*Knox Leader*, 4 August 2009 and *The Age*, 22 August 2009). The remaining two articles in the '*Legal*' category are among only four of the 185 analysed that considered the due process consequences of the banning provisions. The four articles were all published in state-wide newspapers, in the *Herald Sun* on 6 and 7 December 2007, and in *The Sunday Age* on 31 July 2011 and 16 October 2011.

The first two of these articles contained a general discussion of the perceived need for and purpose of the banning provisions, and were published in the *Herald Sun* alongside the passage of the initial legislation through the Victorian Parliament on 6 and 7 December 2007. Their primary focus was the '*Imposition*' of the banning provisions. The only due process consideration noted in these articles related to the proposed amendment to introduce a right of judicial appeal against a banning notice. The underlying tone of each article was critical and implied support for 'drunks' from those supporting a right of appeal.

The remaining two articles that noted the individual rights of recipients were published in *The Sunday Age* in 2011. Each reported the case of a 21 year old woman banned for a year from every pub, bottle shop and licensed restaurant in the city of Swan Hill, Victoria, under separate Liquor Accord provisions of the *LCRA Act 2007* (s146A-D).[48] On 31 July 2011, the first article outlined a pending Supreme Court challenge to police powers under Liquor Accords. On 16 October 2011, the second article detailed the decision by Victoria Police to drop the 12 month ban against the 21 year old. The most significant media comment with respect to the themes considered in this research was published in the 16 October 2011 article, and was made by Mark Woods from the Law Institute of Victoria.

> It's kangaroo justice… The person who makes the complaint against someone makes the decision to exclude them without their reasons or their evidence being tested. (*The Sunday Age*, 16 October 2011)

---

[48]Liquor Accord banning powers do not relate to public spaces and their specific impact upon the right to move freely is much more limited. However, Liquor Accord banning records and related barring order records (under provisions in the *Justice Legislation Amendment Act 2011)*, are not available for examination. The VCGLR confirmed that no data is retained or available for public scrutiny (personal email, 27 June 2014).

This is the only example in any of the 185 articles analysed of a clear connection being made between individual rights and the use of on-the-spot, discretionary police powers to punish. Significantly, this comment was made not in relation to the more expansive police banning notice powers of the *LCRA Act 2007*, but with respect to separate and more limited Liquor Accord provisions, which do not exclude recipients from public spaces.

Across the 185 articles, where a perspective was evident, both the tone and focus presumed a problem of disorderly behaviour in the NTE and the necessity of banning as a solution. The media coverage reflected the parliamentary assumptions, rhetoric and hyperbole in relation to the LCRA Bill 2007 and JLA Bill 2010. Loosely framed, vaguely defined pejorative descriptors were applied to the problematic elements from whom the banning provisions would protect the law-abiding majority. Common terms included 'thugs,' 'louts,' 'drunks,' 'troublemakers,' 'yobbos,' and 'boozers.' The detail of the articles also mirrored the parliamentary discourse. In particular, no meaningful empirical or research evidence was presented in the media articles in support of either the need for the banning provisions or their presumed effectiveness to address issues in the NTE. Anecdotes and specific incidents were used to frame and generalise the issues. For example, the cases of Shannon McCormack, who died after being assaulted in Melbourne's Southbank area, and John Hucker, who was in a coma after a 'schoolies'[49] incident in Lorne on Victoria's Surf Coast, were cited by the *Herald Sun* on 6 December 2007 as evidence of the serious problem that must be addressed. While not in any way diminishing the tragedy of each case, they do not prove a more general issue of alcohol-related disorder in the NTE. Sacco (1995) noted the particularly dramatic value of reporting atypical incidents, and the potential for public issues to be created out of individual experiences.

3.4.2.3 Summary

The media coverage was overwhelmingly supportive of the discretionary police power to ban. The articles repeated many of the assumptions that were evident across the parliamentary debates, about the problem of alcohol-related disorder in the NTE, and the presumed effectiveness of banning as a response. The focus upon specific behaviours and individual events typified the episodic nature of the media coverage of crime (Cheliotis 2010; Surette 2015). There was no acknowledgment or consideration of any underlying societal issues or of the potential consequences of police-imposed banning notices for recipients. In particular, there was no analysis of the erosion of individual rights or procedural protections. The language used across the articles embodied the 'them/us' perspective evident in the parliamentary debates of the banning Bills. The media coverage was similarly based upon fear of the 'dangerous other' (Simon 2007; Drake 2011) engaging in alcohol-related disorder, who

[49]Schoolies take place following the end of year 12 exams, when students typically spend a period of time away from home to mark the completion of their formal schooling.

were demonised and presumed to deserve all they get (Altheide 2006; Beale 2006; Mason 2007).

The media analysis highlights an inherently parliamentary and police perspective (Sacco 1995). The discretionary police-imposed banning notice was reported but its need, effectiveness or the consequential erosion of individual rights were not questioned. There was no meaningful media-driven public critique of the problem that banning was expected to address, or of the effectiveness of the provisions. As well as no effective scrutiny of the powers contained within the banning provisions, there was no media analysis of the published banning notice data. Despite the expectations expressed during parliamentary debates of the LCRA Bill 2007, the published data was not a vehicle for the public scrutiny of the use of the banning provisions. Not only has the data not been published fully, or considered in parliament, but there was no media examination beyond simple statements of numbers of bans issued. It is clear that neither published data nor media coverage has effected any meaningful public scrutiny of the police power to ban.

3.4.3 Judicial Oversight and Public Scrutiny

Judicial oversight, both expressly detailed in Victoria's *Charter Act* and through post hoc judicial review of legislation and the actions of criminal justice agencies, should provide an additional layer of scrutiny for legislative provisions and their application. Judicial oversight includes both statutory interpretation of legislation and review of individual penalties imposed, to ensure ongoing accountability across the criminal justice system. However, there are no court data, legal pronouncements or case law regarding Victoria's banning notice powers. Judicial appeals of other police-imposed penalties, including breach proceedings for banning notices, are typically the responsibility of the Magistracy.[50] To consider the gap in the legitimate public scrutiny of the banning provisions twelve interviews were conducted with Magistrates across Victoria ($n = 12$). The interviews examined the Magistrates' perceptions of police-imposed discretionary justice; their views and experiences of the banning provisions; and their thoughts on the judicial review of banning notices. The objective of each interview was to gather a personal view of these themes. Any perspectives offered relate only to the interview participants and no broader assumptions were made or inferences drawn. The research output has been anonymised and pseudonyms applied. The only identifier used was to discern whether the participant was based in a regional court (MagReg: $n = 7$) or in a metropolitan court (MagMet: $n = 5$) at the

[50] Legislative provisions, and their compliance with the *Charter Act*, are reviewed at Supreme Court level.

time of the interview.[51] The pseudonyms are sequential: MagReg01 to MagReg07, and MagMet01 to MagMet05.

Approximately half of the initial respondents subsequently declined to be interviewed, stating they had no direct knowledge of the banning provisions, and felt unable to provide relevant information or perspectives.[52] This feedback highlighted, for the sample contacted, a notable absence of judicial awareness of the issues embedded within the banning provisions, as well as the lack of judicial oversight of banning per se. One participant, who agreed to be interviewed, noted:

> To tell you the truth, I didn't even know it [police banning powers] existed until I got your request [to be interviewed] and that's damning in itself. (MagReg05)

3.4.3.1 Discretionary Police Powers & Consequences for Due Process

Ten of the twelve participants expressed disquiet about discretionary police powers to ban people from public areas.[53] Common concerns related to the effect of banning notices on due process protections, and accountability of the police use of banning. In an explicit expression of concern about police-imposed discretionary powers, MagReg03 stated: "I think it's an intrusion on the effective administration of the criminal justice system… I just think it's appallingly excessive". MagMet02 noted that discretionary summary justice risked reducing accountability of police decision-making: "Potentially. There would have to be, within that [discretionary police powers], a lack of accountability".

Within a lengthy consideration of how discretionary police powers to punish are opaque to public scrutiny and of their effect upon the individual rights of recipients, MagReg05 outlined the risks of over-zealous and arbitrary application of banning notices.

> … those sorts of powers, arbitrary powers, are becoming more remote in terms of public scrutiny. At least if a person goes through the court the public has a chance to come and look, and understand what's happened. Whereas an incident might be dealt with on the scene by a police officer… it's out of the view of the public. It's not under public scrutiny. I suppose that's the reservation I have. It means that we all have to trust that people of good faith are operating these powers and exercising these powers… If they are exercised zealously to the very letter, I can see there could be some human rights infringed and that would concern me… I suppose that we just need to hasten slowly in the powers that we exercise arbitrarily. If you look at the entirety of the power, banning someone from an area is a fairly significant power. What concerns me is if it is exercised in a situation where both parties are in a state of heightened emotion… whether that power is exercised in the cool light of day or is an emotional response to the situation. (MagReg05)

---

[51] This detail was recorded to discern any differences in the views of Magistrates based primarily in regional and metropolitan courts. The work conducted in each court is comparable, but metropolitan courts are typically busier.

[52] If a Magistrate had no knowledge of the banning notices, the researcher did not provide any information or offer any explanation.

[53] The remaining two preferred not to offer a view.

Adding to a general concern about discretionary police powers, and with an explicit reference to notions of balance in the administration of justice, MagMet01 noted

> ... on a cost/benefit balancing exercise, in terms of public safety and law and order, it [a banning notice] may be justified, but there is the potential for abuse there.

A link between the due process protections of individual recipients, and the vulnerability this creates in the appropriate imposition of bans was also perceived by MagReg01.

> Obviously there is [impact upon due process protections]... Without there being any judicial scrutiny we have to rely on the good conscience and morality of the police officers that impose it [banning notice].

The possibility that a banning notice may be imposed incorrectly was acknowledged by MagMet05: "It may be unfortunate that someone is sucked into that vortex who is innocent".

While conceding no knowledge of actual abuses of banning notice powers, MagReg02 noted the risks within a police-imposed power that is not subject to judicial scrutiny: "It places enormous responsibility on the police and if you have relatively junior police with these powers it might be a cause for concern".

Across this sample of Magistrates clear concern was expressed about the potential for abuse and the inappropriate application of discretionary police powers. These were perceptions, but the findings, combined with the absence of judicial oversight and the lack of public scrutiny of police decisions to impose banning notices, serve to reinforce documented concern about police-imposed discretionary justice (Spooner 2001; Zedner 2005; Walsh and Taylor 2006, 2007; Beckett and Herbert 2010a).

3.4.3.2 The Right of Judicial Appeal

The interview participants considered the significance of the absence of a right of court-based appeal against the imposition of a police-imposed banning notice, and how this could affect meaningful scrutiny of these provisions. They were asked whether recipients should have the opportunity to seek a judicial or independent appeal of a police decision to issue a banning notice.

None of the Magistrates interviewed opposed a notional right of appeal. MagReg03 was unequivocal and stated that "absolutely" a right of appeal should exist. MagReg05 linked the right of appeal to other types of infringement penalty, and directly referenced the pre-emptive nature of banning notices as a reason why appeal provisions were necessary: "Especially in the pre-emptive or anticipatory sense, then that should be able to be challenged I would have thought".

That banning notices limit individual rights and the possibility that police officers may impose a ban mistakenly, were offered by two Magistrates (MagMet03 and MagMet02) as justifications for the right of appeal. The immediate nature of the banning notice penalty was also cited, by MagMet06, as a key reason why it should be subject to review. A more general perspective was provided by MagMet01 who articulated support for the court-based appeal of banning notices, but offered no specific reasoning or rationale.

There were two primary objections to a right of appeal against the imposition of a banning notice presented during parliamentary debates of the LCRA Bill 2007. Firstly, that an appeal was impractical, would delay the implementation of the punishment, and therefore reduce the ability of Victoria Police to control alcohol-related disorder in the NTE. Secondly, that an appeal would require police officers to complete additional paperwork, to document evidence and record witnesses (Legislative Assembly 2007b, c, d; Legislative Council 2007a, b). Neither of these concerns were raised by the Magistrates who were interviewed.

MagReg05 acknowledged having no prior knowledge of the police-imposed banning notice powers when made aware of the research interviews. Having examined the provisions themselves, MagReg05 expressed concern that the way in which the *LCRA Act 2007* was framed created the subjective and arbitrary nature of what constituted a 'need' for a banning notice. MagReg05 noted that the pre-emptive capacity of the banning provisions, which may be imposed for behaviours that are not objectively assessed, when combined with the absence of independent review, significantly undermined the due process protections of banning notice recipients.

3.4.3.3 The Extension of the Banning Provisions to 72 h

The interview participants were asked to consider the 2010 increase in the permitted length of a banning notice from 24 to 72 h. No Magistrate declared their support for the extension to 72 h, but there were three clearly critical responses. Two Magistrates, MagMet02 and MagReg06, questioned the effectiveness of the increase. MagMet03 noted that longer bans were not likely to address problematic behaviours: "… there's not much point to that really… For me that's not really going to achieve a great deal in terms of addressing behaviours".

The extension to 72 h was considered by some Magistrates in the context of typical drinking patterns. A three day ban was not believed to reflect the usual weekend to weekend nature of alcohol consumption in the NTE.

> As a concept [72 h police-imposed banning notices], I don't think it is effective at all. I don't understand what three days results in… people don't drink on a three day cycle. It's weekend to weekend; three days is not going to have much impact at all. (MagMet02)

MagReg05 regarded 72 h as a long time: "…it seems a long time to me to order someone away from an area…" During discussion of the extension of banning notices to 72 h, both MagMet02 and MagReg06 expressed doubt about the enforceability of banning notices, and their effectiveness as a mechanism to control alcohol-related disorder. MagMet02 perceived that bans were not taken particularly seriously and that they are easy to breach.

> If you just keep your head down and head back into the city, the police don't stop and search anybody. I really don't know that people are that scared anyway. (MagMet02)

MagReg06 questioned both the rationale for the imposition of a banning notice, and the effectiveness of ban enforcement activities.

> Typically, limited thought is given to their imposition. They can be an effective option, but enforcement is an issue; both how likely it is and how thorough it is. (MagReg06)

MagMet01 noted that banning notices "are not enforceable unless they [someone breaching a ban] are caught". Addressed in the context of the extension of banning notices to 72 h, there was some concern regarding the rationale for longer bans, and acknowledgment that their use and effectiveness was not subject to sufficient scrutiny.

3.4.3.4 Banning as a Punishment or for Community Protection?

Opinion was divided regarding the primary function of banning notices. Punishment was stated by six Magistrates (half of the sample) as being a core purpose or result of a banning notice. Within the responses that considered banning notices to be a punishment, the strength of feeling ranged from absolute to more complex, multi-dimensional perspectives. The strongest belief that banning notices are a punishment was offered by MagReg04, who considered them to be "… a significant sanction and a punishment." MagReg01 agreed and categorised banning notices as "primarily punishment."

Other participants balanced the punishment aspect with other factors. MagReg05 combined punishment with a method of controlling problematic behaviours.

> I suppose I can see it [a banning notice] would be imposed as a way of controlling behaviour, but I think there is a punishment aspect to it. (MagReg05)

A similar view was provided by MagMet03, who noted the deterrent effect for both recipients and for the broader community.

> I think there are elements of deterrence, but the question of punishment is in there as well…those conditions [of a banning notice] do have a punitive effect… (MagMet03)

Strong opinions were also articulated that disagreed with banning notices being viewed as a punishment. MagMet02 focused on their protective purpose and dismissed the punishment perspective: "Protect the public. I don't see it as a punishment, no." MagReg03 agreed with the protective priority of banning notices, and regarded them as

> primarily a way of protecting the wider community from drunken violence, usually on Saturday nights. (MagReg03)

MagMet01 felt that a banning notice is not a significant penalty and categorised them as a mechanism to protect the community enjoying the NTE.

> My primary focus would be on public safety. I would prefer to leave the punitive aspect. I think to most people not being able to go to a particular area or premises is not a significant penalty…. Particularly in places like Melbourne I think there's a public safety drive more

> than a punitive element. I would hope that there is no punitive element to it because that should be subject to judicial oversight - it should all be focused on public safety. (MagMet01)

None of the Magistrates interviewed had conducted breach proceedings of a police-imposed banning notice. Most had included a banning component of some sort as a condition of bail. MagReg05 discussed how banning is applied to bail, citing the examples of family violence and persistent theft which may lead to exclusion from stated locations for the duration of the bail period. Despite bail hearings affording due process rights to defendants, MagReg05 offered a highly pertinent perspective.

> The way I look at it there has to be a good reason. You are infringing on someone's human rights. You have to make sure there is no draconian aspect to it. (MagReg05)

The limited scope of the published banning notice data and the restricted media coverage of banning notices contributes to the lack of accountability and ongoing scrutiny of the banning provisions. These limitations, and the issues to which they lead, were identified by the Magistrates interviewed for this study. Significantly, the discretionary police power to impose banning notices was a source of concern among the interviewees. Without effective judicial oversight of the banning notice provisions, the implications for police legitimacy and for the protection of individual due process rights are considerable. The perspectives offered by this sample of Magistrates differed significantly from the assumptions and expectations that predominated during the parliamentary debates of the banning notice Bills.

3.5 Summary

The analysis in this chapter demonstrates that, despite their tangible consequences for individual rights, there has been very little meaningful pre- or post-enactment scrutiny of the banning notice provisions. *Charter Act* compliance processes were diluted and parliamentary rhetoric presumed the existence of a problem and assumed the appropriateness of banning to address it.

Limitations in the published banning notice data are evident, with insufficient detail to enable meaningful analysis and mandated requirements missing. The data recording the Indigenous status of banning notice recipients is flawed and does not enable accurate assessment of the effect of banning upon Indigenous Victorians. Furthermore, the published data has not been subject to parliamentary analysis, despite expectations noted in 2007 that the data would ensure public scrutiny and appropriate use of the banning notice provisions. This is despite the opportunity presented by the extension of the banning notice powers under the JLA Bill 2010. No consideration of the published data was evident during parliamentary debates of the JLA Bill 2010, or since.

Despite notable media coverage of the imposition and use of banning notices, and of associated issues relating to the NTE, only four of the 185 articles examined made any reference to issues regarding the use of banning notices. There has been no meaningful media analysis of the broader consequences of the provisions, of their effect upon individual rights or the potential misuse of discretionary police powers to ban. This aspect of the public scrutiny of the legislation has been non-existent.

There has also been no judicial oversight of the way in which individual notices have been imposed and no opportunity for the banning provisions, or their consequential erosion of the due process rights of individual recipients, to be legally reviewed. The ongoing parliamentary and media failure to examine the formally published banning notice data, media indifference to the effect of banning upon individual rights, and an absence of independent oversight, combine with judicial concern about the risks and expansion of discretionary police powers to punish. These findings compound the issues emanating from the shortcomings identified in the parliamentary scrutiny of the banning Bills. They confirm Crawford's (2009) concern about the lack of meaningful analysis of discretionary police powers. There has been no effective scrutiny of banning as a matter of police practice, public debate or jurisprudence. Balance is not evident in the imposition, scrutiny or enduring impact of banning notices.

References

Altheide, D. (2006). The mass media, crime and terrorism. *Journal of International Criminal Justice, 4,* 982–997.

Ashworth, A. (2006). *Principles of criminal law* (5th ed.). Oxford: Oxford University Press.

Australian Bureau of Statistics (ABS). (2006). *Population distribution, aboriginal and torres strait islander Australians*, 2006. [Online]: ABS. Retrieved from http://www.abs.gov.au/ausstats/abs@.nsf/mf/4705.0.

Australian Bureau of Statistics (ABS). (2011). *Census of population and housing—counts of aboriginal and torres strait islander Australians*, 2011. [Online]: ABS. Retrieved from http://www.abs.gov.au/ausstats/abs@.nsf/Lookup/2075.0main+features42011.

Australian Bureau of Statistics (ABS). (2013). *2011 Census Quick Stats*. [Online]: ABS. Retrieved from http://www.abs.gov.au/websitedbs/censushome.nsf/home/quickstats.

Australian Human Rights Commission (AHRC). (2009). *Submission to National human rights consultation*. Sydney: AHRC.

Bartels, L., & Richards, K. (Eds.). (2011). *Qualitative criminology: Stories from the field*. Sydney: Hawkins Press.

Beale, S. (2006). The news medias influence on criminal justice policy: How market-driven news promotes punitiveness. *William & Mary Law Review, 48,* 397–481.

Beckett, K., & Herbert, S. (2008). Dealing with disorder: Social control in the post-industrial city. *Theoretical Criminology, 12*(1), 5–30.

Beckett, K., & Herbert, S. (2009). Zoning out disorder: Assessing contemporary practices of urban social control. *New Perspectives on Crime and Criminal Justice, 47,* 1–25.

Beckett, K., & Herbert, S. (2010a). *Banished. The new social control in Urban America*. New York: Oxford University Press.

Beckett, K., & Herbert, S. (2010b). Penal boundaries; Banishment and the expansion of punishment. *Law & Social Inquiry, 35*(1), 1–38.

Cheliotis, L. K. (2010). The ambivalent consequences of visibility: Crime and prisons in the mass media. *Crime, Media, Culture, 6*(2), 169–184.

Chibnall, S. (2001). *Law-and-order news* (Reissued ed.). Abingdon, Oxon: Routledge.

Commissioner, Chief. (2008). *Annual report on banning notices: Issued under S148R liquor control reform amendment act 2007*. Melbourne: Victoria Police.
Chief Commissioner. (2009). *Annual report by the chief commissioner victoria police (2009). Liquor control reform act 1998, Section 148R*. Melbourne: Victoria Police.
Chief Commissioner. (2010). *Annual report by the chief commissioner victoria police (2010). Liquor control reform act 1998, Section 148R*. Melbourne: Victoria Police.
Chief Commissioner. (2011). *2010–2011 Annual report by the chief commissioner victoria police. Section 148R (Banning notices and exclusion orders)*. Melbourne: Victoria Police.
Chief Commissioner. (2012). *2011–2012 Annual Report by the Chief Commissioner of Victoria Police. Section 148R (Banning Notices and Exclusion Orders)*. Melbourne: Victoria Police.
Chief Commissioner. (2013). *2012–2013 Annual report by the chief commissioner of victoria police. Section 148R (Banning Notices and Exclusion Orders)*. Melbourne: Victoria Police.
Chief Commissioner. (2014). *2013–2014 Annual report by the chief commissioner of victoria police. Section 148R (Banning Notices and Exclusion Orders)*. Melbourne: Victoria Police.
Chief Commissioner. (2015). *2014–2015 Annual report by the chief commissioner of victoria police. Section 148R (Banning Notices and Exclusion Orders)*. Melbourne: Victoria Police.
Chief Commissioner. (2016). *2015–2016 Annual report by the chief commissioner of victoria police. Section 148R (Banning Notices and Exclusion Orders)*. Melbourne: Victoria Police.
Chilton, P. A. (2004). *Analysing political discourse: Theory and practice*. London: Routledge.
Crawford, A. (2009). Governing through anti-social behaviour: Regulatory challenges to criminal justice. *British Journal of Criminology, 49*(6), 810–831.
Crawford, A. (2013). 'Sticks and carrots and sermons': Some thoughts on compliance and legitimacy in the regulation of youth anti-social behaviour. In A. Crawford & A. Hucklesby (Eds.), *Legitimacy and compliance in criminal justice* (pp. 181–214). Abingdon, Oxon: Routledge.
Crawford, A., & Lister, S. (2007). *The use and impact of dispersal orders*. Bristol: Joseph Rowntree Foundation.
Crofts, T., & Mitchell, T. (2011). Prohibited behaviour orders and indigenous overrepresentation in the criminal justice system. *Current Issues in Criminal Justice, 23*(2), 277–285.
Cunneen, C. (2001). *Conflict, politics and crime: Aboriginal communities and police*. Sydney: Allen & Unwin.
Department of Justice, Victoria. (2008a). *Victoria's alcohol action plan: 2008–2013*. Melbourne: State Government of Victoria.
Department of Justice, Victoria. (2008b). *Charter of human rights and responsibilities; guidelines for legislation and policy officers in Victoria*. Melbourne: Human Rights Unit, State Government of Victoria.
Drake, D. (2011). The 'dangerous other' in maximum-security prisons. *Criminology & Criminal Justice, 11*(4), 367–383.
Drugs and Crime Prevention Committee (DCPC). (2001). *Reporting crime in the Melbourne central business district*. Melbourne: Parliament of Victoria.
Drugs and Crime Prevention Committee (DCPC). (2010). *Inquiry into strategies to reduce assaults in public places in Victoria*. Melbourne: Parliament of Victoria.
Duff, R. A. (2011). Responsibility, citizenship and criminal law. In R. A Duff & S. P Green (Eds.), *Philosophical foundations of criminal law* (pp. 125–150). Oxford: Oxford University Press.
Farmer, C. (2014). Is a 24-hour ban such a bad thing? *Australian Journal of Human Rights, 20*(2), 39–62.
Farmer, C. (2016). Victoria's banning notice provisions: Parliamentary, procedural and individual vulnerabilities. *Journal of Criminological Research, Policy & Practice, 2*(3), 173–184.
Farmer, C. (2017a). The disparity between human rights policy and parliamentary practice in Australia: A victorian case study. *The International Journal of Human Rights, 27*(2), 167–188.
Farmer, C. (2017b). Upholding whose right? Discretionary police powers to punish, collective 'pre-victimisation' and the dilution of individual rights. *Australian & New Zealand Journal of Criminology, 50*(4), 493–509.
Finkelstein, C. (2003). Is risk a harm? *University of Pennsylvania Law Review, 151*, 963–1001.

Gelb, K. (2006). *Myths and misconceptions: Public opinion versus public judgment about sentencing*. Melbourne: Sentencing Advisory Council, Victoria.
Golder, B., & Williams, G. (2007). Balancing national security and human rights: assessing the legal response of common law nations to the threat of terrorism. *Journal of Comparative Policy Analysis: Research and Practice, 8*(1), 43–62.
Goodey, J. (2006). Ethnic profiling, criminal (In) justice and minority populations. *Critical Criminology, 14,* 207–212.
Grossman, M., Bruck, D., Stephenson, P., Dwyer, R., & Roose, J. (2013). *Learning to engage: A review of Victoria police cross-cultural training practices*. Melbourne: Victoria University.
Hadfield, P., Lister, S., & Traynor, P. (2009). 'This town's a different town today': Policing and regulating the night-time economy. *Criminology & Criminal Justice: An International Journal, 9*(4), 465–485.
Hall, S., Critcher, C., Jefferson, T., Clarke, J., & Roberts, B. (1978). *Policing the crisis: Mugging, the state, and law and order*. London: The MacMillan Press Ltd.
Hallsworth, S. (2006). Racial targeting and social control: Looking behind the police. *Critical Criminology, 14*, 293–311.
Harris, D. A. (2006). US experiences with racial and ethnic profiling: History, current issues and the future. *Critical Criminology, 14*, 213–239.
Hart, C., Rymes, B., Souto-Manning, M., Brown, C., & Luke, A. (2005). Analysing political discourse: Toward a cognitive approach. *Critical Discourse Studies, 2*(2), 189–201.
Hennink, M., Hutter, I., & Bailey, A. (2011). *Qualitative research methods*. London: Sage Publications.
Johnston, E. (1991). *Royal commission into aboriginal deaths in custody: National reports*. Canberra: Australian Government Publishing Service.
Jones, D., & Wolfe, M. (2010). Public policy and the mass media: An information processing approach. In S. Koch-Baumgartner & L. Voltmer (Eds.), *Public policy and mass media: The interplay of mass communication and political decision making* (pp. 17–43). London: Routledge.
Jupp, V., Davies, P., & Francis, P. (2000). *Doing criminological research*. London: Sage Publications.
Kidd-Hewitt, D. (1995). Crime and the media: A criminological perspective. In D. Kidd-Hewitt & R. Osborne (Eds.), *Crime and the media: The post-modern spectacle* (pp. 9–24). London: Pluto Press.
Krippendorff, K. (2004). *Content analysis: An introduction to its methodology*. London: Sage Publications.
Lowry, D. T., Nio, T. C. J., & Leitner, D. W. (2003). Setting the public fear agenda: A longitudinal analysis of network TV crime reporting, public perceptions of crime, and FBI crime statistics. *Journal of Communication, 53*(1), 61–73.
Luke, G., & Cunneen, C. (1995). Discretionary decisions in juvenile justice and the criminalisation of indigenous young people. *Youth Studies Australia, 14*(4), 38–46.
Mason, P. (2007). Misinformation, myth and distortion: How the press construct imprisonment in Britain. *Journalism Studies, 8*(3), 481–496.
May, T. (2001). *Social research: Issues, methods and process*. Maidenhead, Berks: Open University Press.
Mazerolle, L., Bennett, S., Davis, J., Sargeant, E., & Manning, M. (2013). Legitimacy in policing: A systematic review. *Campbell Systematic Reviews, 1,* 1–146.
McCombs, M. (2004). *Setting the agenda: The mass media and public opinion*. Cambridge: UK Polity Press.
Oberdiek, J. (2009). Towards a right against risking. *Law and Philosophy, 28*(4), 367–392.
O'Brien, M. (2011a). *Media release: New designated area in Dandenong adds to Coalition Govt blitz on booze-fuelled crime*. Melbourne: State Government Victoria.
O'Brien, M. (2011b). *Media release: Docklands declared designated area to tackle anti-social behaviour*. Melbourne: State Government Victoria.
Paradies, Y. (2005). Anti-racism and indigenous Australians. *Analyses of Social Issues and Public Policy, 5*(1), 1–28.

Parliament of Victoria. (n.d.). *About parliament*. [Online]: Parliament of Victoria. Retrieved from http://www.parliament.vic.gov.au/about.

Patton, M. Q. (1990). *Qualitative evaluation and research methods*. Newbury Park, California: Sage Publications.

Rares, S. (2013). *Legality, rights and statutory interpretation*. Paper presented at the AGS Administrative Law Conference, Canberra.

Riffe, D., Lacy, S., & Fico, F. G. (2005). *Analysing media messages: Using quantitative content analysis in research*. London: LEA.

Roberts, L., & Indermaur, D. (2009). What Australians think about crime and justice: Results from the 2007 Survey of Social Attitudes. *AIC Reports: Research and Public Policy Series 101*. Canberra: AIC.

Sacco, V. F. (1995). Reactions to crime and violence. *Annals of the American Academy of Political and Social Science, 539*, 141–154.

Saunders, B., Eriksson, A., Lansdell, G., & Brown, M. (2013). *An examination of the impact of unpaid infringement notices on disadvantaged groups and the criminal justice system—towards a best practice model*. Melbourne: Criminal Justice Research Consortium, Monash University.

Schreier, M. (2012). *Qualitative content analysis in practice*. London: Sage Publications.

Scrutiny of Acts & Regulations Committee, Victoria (SARC). (2010). *SARC alert digest No. 14 of 2010*. Melbourne: State Government of Victoria.

Scrutiny of Acts & Regulations Committee, Victoria (SARC). (2011). *Review of the charter of human rights and responsibilities act 2006*. Melbourne: State Government of Victoria.

Silverman, J. (2012). *Crime, policy and the media: The shaping of criminal justice, 1989–2010*. London: Routledge.

Simon, J. (2007). *Governing through crime: How the war on crime transformed American democracy and created a culture of fear*. New York: Oxford University Press.

Sivasubramaniam, D., & Goodman-Delahunty, J. (2008). Ethnicity and trust: Perceptions of police bias. *International Journal of Police Sciences & Management, 10*, 388–440.

Spooner, P. (2001). 'Moving in the wrong direction': An analysis of police move-on powers in Queensland. *Youth Studies Australia, 20*(1), 27–31.

Surette, R. (2015). *Media, crime and criminal justice* (5th ed.). Stamford, CT: Cengage Learning.

Tyler, T. R., & Wakslak, C. J. (2004). Profiling and police legitimacy: Procedural justice, attributions of motive, and acceptance of police authority. *Criminology, 42*(2), 253–281.

Van Dijk, T. A. (1993). Principles of critical discourse analysis. *Discourse & Society, 4*(2), 249–283.

Victoria Police. (2003). *Crime statistics: 2002–2003*. Melbourne: Victoria Police.

Victoria Police. (2004). *Crime statistics: 2003–2004*. Melbourne: Victoria Police.

Victoria Police. (2005). *Crime statistics: 2004–2005*. Melbourne: Victoria Police.

Victoria Police. (2006). *Crime Statistics: 2005–2006*. Melbourne: Victoria Police.

Victoria Police. (2007). *Crime statistics: 2006–2007*. Melbourne: Victoria Police.

Victoria Police. (2008). *Crime statistics: 2007–2008*. Melbourne: Victoria Police.

Victoria Police. (2012). *Crime statistics: 2011–2012*. Melbourne: Victoria Police.

Victoria Police. (2013). *Equality is not the same. Victoria Police response to community consultation and reviews on field contact policy and data collection and cross cultural training*. Melbourne: Victoria Police.

Victorian Commission for Gambling and Liquor Licensing (VCGLR). (2017). *Designated areas*. [Online]: VCGLR. Retrieved from http://www.vcglr.vic.gov.au/utility/community/government+initiatives/designated+areas/designated_areas.

Waldron, J. (2003). Security and liberty: The image of balance. *The Journal of Political Philosophy, 11*(2), 191–210.

Walsh, T., & Taylor, M. (2006). *Nowhere to go: The impact of police move-on powers on homeless people in Queensland*. Brisbane: Queensland Public Interest Law Clearing House.

Walsh, T., & Taylor, M. (2007). 'You're not welcome here': Police move-on powers and discrimination law. *University of New South Wales Law Journal, 30*, 151–173.

Weatherspoon, F. D. (2004). Racial profiling of African-American males: Stopped, searched and stripped of constitutional protection. *The John Marshall Law Review, 38*(2), 439–468.

Weitzer, R., & Tuch, S. A. (2002). Perceptions of racial profiling: Race, class and personal experience. *Criminology, 40*(2), 435–456.

Yesufu, S. (2013). Discriminatory use of police stop and search powers in London, UK. *International Journal of Police Sciences & Management, 15*(4), 281–293.

Young, R. (2010). Ethnic profiling and summary justice—An ominous silence. In K. Sveinsson (Ed.), *Ethnic profiling: The use of 'Race' in UK Law enforcement* (pp. 43–9). London: Runnymede Trust.

Zedner, L. (2005). Securing liberty in the face of terror; reflections from criminal justice. *Journal of Law and Society, 32*(4), 507–533.

Zedner, L. (2007a). Preventive justice or pre-punishment? The case of control orders. *Current Legal Problems, 60*(1), 174–2003.

Zedner, L. (2007b). Seeking security by eroding rights: The side-stepping of due process. In B. Goold & L. Lazarus (Eds.), *Security and human rights* (pp. 257–275). Oxford: Hart Publishing.

Zedner, L. (2007c). Pre-crime and post-criminology? *Theoretical Criminology, 11*(2), 261–281.

Hansard

Legislative Assembly. (2007a). *State of Victoria parliamentary debates* (Hansard), Book 15, November 1, pp. 3818–21.

Legislative Assembly. (2007b). *State of Victoria parliamentary debates* (Hansard), Book 16, November 21, pp. 3998–4008.

Legislative Assembly. (2007c). *State of Victoria parliamentary debates* (Hansard), Book 16, November 22, pp. 4067–87.

Legislative Assembly. (2007d). *State of Victoria parliamentary debates* (Hansard), Book 17, December 6, pp. 4401–12.

Legislative Assembly. (2010a). *State of Victoria parliamentary debates* (Hansard), Book 4, March 25, pp. 1127–1135.

Legislative Council. (2007a). *State of Victoria parliamentary debates* (Hansard), Book 17, December 5, pp. 3861–899.

Legislative Council. (2007b). *State of Victoria parliamentary debates* (Hansard), Book 17, December 6, pp. 4003–05.

Legislative Council. (2010). *State of Victoria parliamentary debates* (Hansard), Book 6, May 6, pp. 1810–1820.

Chapter 4
The 'Problem' of Victoria's Banning Notice Provisions

Abstract This final chapter draws together the key findings from the research. It highlights the incongruity between claims made to secure the passage of Victoria's police-imposed banning provisions, and the absence of ongoing scrutiny and analysis of their use. While the actual effect of banning upon undesirable behaviours in the night-time economy is not sufficiently monitored or understood, the consequences for the separation of powers and the individual rights of recipients are clear. The dissonance between the assumptions and language used to justify the need for police powers to ban and the broader consequences of the absence of meaningful oversight is significant. The specific findings in relation to Victoria's banning notices epitomise core concerns about pre-emptive and preventive justice, which have been expressed across a range of international contexts.

Balance is an implicit dimension of the way in which laws in Western legal traditions are enacted, interpreted and enforced, through mechanisms such as the separation of powers and due process safeguards. However, manifestations of balance are not fixed or uniform. Within criminal justice processes the fluidity of how balance operates in practice is exemplified through the shifting emphasis on individual rights, community protection and notions of victimisation. This is reinforced by evolving theoretical constructs, such as Packer's (1964, 1968) depiction of crime control and due process, Dubber's (2002, 2005, 2006, 2011) police power model, Roach's (1999) conception of punitive and non-punitive victims' rights, and the human rights models of, among others, Ashworth (2004a, b, 2006), Ashworth and Zedner (2008), Ashworth and Redmayne (2010) and Dripps (2011).[1] These theoretical models demonstrate the difficulty of balancing the conflicting demands of the due process rights of defendants, the expectations of victims of crime, and a collective need for community safety.

The application of criminal justice models reflects a complex evolution of public, political, operational policing and judicial priorities. Despite an emerging interplay of human rights charters and rights-based models, these theoretical concepts have been undermined by significant legislative developments that expand police discre-

[1]Other models of the criminal process are acknowledged, such as Llewellyn's (1962) parental and arm's length models, and the hierarchical and co-ordinate models depicted by Damaska (1975), which align broadly with European and Anglo-American traditions.

C. Farmer, *Discretionary Police Powers to Punish*, SpringerBriefs in Criminology,
https://doi.org/10.1007/978-981-10-8869-8_4

tion, enhance pre-emption, and lower thresholds of behaviour classified as criminal. Police discretionary powers to punish reduce the cost and increase the efficiency of administering justice, but typically at the expense of individual rights. Key research and theoretical literature across a range of criminological contexts has drawn attention to constructions of 'balance' in the provision of justice.[2] Balance suggests a sense of equilibrium, with a legislative and judicial commitment to parity between defendants' due process protections, and the needs of both victims of crime and the broader community. Changes to the criminal process in recent decades have reflected a dilution of defendants' due process rights, and a 're-balancing' towards the primacy of risk mitigation and public protection. Embedded within this shift is a subordination of the rights of the accused to the needs of potential victims within the law-abiding majority.

Victoria's banning notice powers embody many of the recent initiatives that 're-balance' collective security away from the due process rights of alleged offenders. The banning provisions involve a discretionary police decision to punish through exclusion from public spaces, and may be given pre-emptively or in anticipation of a subjectively assessed future behaviour. Banning notices prohibit the lawful action of being in a public place, with an underlying justification of community protection to obviate the risk of victimisation. However, there is a clear dichotomy between the protections enshrined in Victoria's *Charter Act* and a police-imposed pre-emptive summary power to punish by exclusion. Banning notices undermine the due process rights of recipients as they are issued on-the-spot by police officers, take effect immediately, embody a presumption of guilt, can be imposed before the commission of an offence, and require no evidence to be recorded. There is no judicial scrutiny of whether the banning legislation complies with Charter rights, and a police decision to issue a banning notice is not subject to a court-based or any independent appeal. The *Charter Act* appears to have been circumvented by ministerial Statements of Compatibility that authorise a notable addition to police powers at the expense of individual rights.

Through an examination of the way in which Victoria's banning notice provisions were enacted, analysis of the presumptions and justifications used to support the passage of the provisions through parliament, and consideration of the ongoing scrutiny of the police power to ban, it is evident that these discretionary police powers to punish undermine the notion of 'balance' under Victorian criminal and liquor control laws. There is a mismatch between the claims made to justify the introduction of police-imposed banning notices, and the failure to adequately monitor their consequences and effect. Despite the absence of any evidence that banning is an effective deterrent, punishment or behaviour control mechanism, similar measures have since been introduced across nearly all Australian jurisdictions (Farmer et al. 2017).[3] The rationale applied to each subsequent jurisdiction mirrors that used in Vic-

[2]Examples include Ashworth (1996, 2004b), Zedner (2002, 2003, 2005, 2007a, b, c, 2014), Waldron (2003), Tonry (2003), Michaelsen (2005, 2006, 2010), Williams (2006, 2007a, b), Neocleous (2007), Ashworth and Zedner (2008), Bronitt (2008), and Pue (2008).

[3]The Australian Capital Territory (ACT) is the only jurisdiction without such provisions.

toria, and similar issues are evident with respect to a lack of meaningful monitoring and assessment.

This book has demonstrated flaws and omissions in the underlying rationale for Victoria's banning notice provisions, and deficiencies in the nature and extent of the ongoing scrutiny of their use. It is conceivable that police-imposed banning notices have had a positive effect upon behaviours in the night-time economy, both from the perspective of an individual deterrent for recipients and a more general deterrent for the wider community. However, no analysis has been undertaken to identify or to assess the actual effect of banning.[4] Furthermore, in Victoria, and other Australian jurisdictions where police-imposed banning provisions have been introduced, they typically form part of a suite of responses to address alcohol-related behavourial concerns. In the context of multi-faceted provisions, the particular effects of individual reforms are difficult to isolate (Menendez et al. 2015; Miller et al. 2014, 2016). This analytical challenge is exacerbated when the perceived success of an overall strategy is used to justify extensions to the scope or remit of an individual mechanism—as has been the case with banning provisions across Australian jurisdictions (Farmer et al. 2017).

Despite the acknowledged challenges, focused research is essential to understand the range of possible effects of measures to ban individuals from public spaces. It is clear from the published data in Victoria that the consequences for vulnerable recipients of police-imposed bans must be examined closely. The move away from accurately recording the indigeneity of recipients is a particular concern.[5] In addition, as the banning notice documentation includes a 'no fixed abode' option, it would be a simple addition to add this metric to the published data. This would enable the effect of public area banning upon homeless Victorians to be monitored. Beyond analysing the data that is published, a range of mechanisms are required to review the effect of Victoria's police-imposed bans. One method could be to interview recipients of banning notices to understand the effect of the notice upon their short and longer term behaviours, and possible wider consequences for their social networks. Privacy rights preclude the publication of the names of ban recipients in Victoria,[6] and there are ethical challenges inherent in gaining access to this information as well as conducting an appropriate sample of interviews. Nevetheless, recipient interviews would be an essential part of an examination of the effect of banning notices. Curtis et al. (2018) undertook a preliminary assessment of the potential broader deterrent effect of banning, by using a limited online survey to gain an understanding of the level of public awareness of Victoria's banning provisions. Effective assessment of the general deterrent effect of banning will require a more expansive and ongoing study.

[4]Curtis et al. (2018) provides a preliminary consideration of the potential deterrent effect of banning provisions in Victoria.

[5]The data regarding vulnerable recipients of Victoria's banning notices is set out in Sect. 3.4.1b.

[6]Unlike Western Australia, where the names, photographs and town/suburb of residence of Prohibition Order (*Liquor Control Act* 1988) and Probihited Behaviour Order (*Prohibited Behaviour Order Act* 2010) recipients are published online. These orders replicate aspects of Victoria's banning notices, but are not identical provisions.

Other avenues of enquiry could include examining data derived from ID scanners[7] to analyse the nature and extent to which banned patrons are prevented from entering licensed venues, and interviewing police officers and magistrates about their use and experience of the banning provisions.

While the actual effect of banning upon behaviour is not sufficiently understood, the consequences for the separation of powers and the individual rights of recipients are clear. The assumptions and rhetoric used to justify discretionary, pre-emptive police powers to punish, and the lack of meaningful oversight are significant and concerning. The specific findings in relation to Victoria's banning notices exemplify concerns regarding pre-emptive and preventive justice across a range of contexts. For example, in 2016 the government of New South Wales passed legislation expanding police powers to stop, search and detain, permitting police officers to prevent protests based upon subjective assessments of risk, and allowing senior police officers (rather than a judge) to impose public safety orders prohibiting an individual from entering a specified place for up to 72 h.[8] More recently, in Victoria, a proposed tightening of anti-terror laws would permit preventative detention for up to four days without a court order (Andrews 2017).

The balance between police powers, individual rights and community safety is a central focus of this study. Victoria's banning provisions circumvent the separation of powers doctrine, and undermine individual due process protections that should be assured under the *Charter Act*. However, the legislation has not been subject to judicial scrutiny and there is no facility for recipients to appeal their police-imposed ban in court.[9] The assumptions that underpinned the parliamentary rhetoric used to support the banning notice measures, and the way in which their passage through the *Charter Act* requirements was secured, are problematic. The nature and extent of parliamentary analysis of the 'problem', and of the presumed efficacy of the 'solution' were limited. Victoria's banning provisions appear to have been driven by a reactive political desire to be seen to do something in response to a perceived concern, without sufficient empirical evidence to support the 'need' or thorough consideration of any potential consequences for individual rights (Crawford 2013). Rather than ensuring an effective balance for all members of the community, banning notices circumvent the core due process rights of alleged offenders. The rights of a police-determined undesirable minority are subsumed to a politically proclaimed need to protect the wider community, in response to politically-driven, but largely unsubstantiated, fear.

Of course, there are reasonable arguments which can be presented to support the expansion of police-imposed summary justice, across a range of contexts. Such justifications typically prioritise risk and the need for the wider community to feel, if not necessarily to demonstrably be, safe. It is possible that in certain circumstances,

---

[7]In Queensland, for example, ID scanners at licensed venues link to a wider system which enables a prospective patron's ID to be cross-checked against a database of people in receipt of banning orders.

[8]As an amendment to the *Law Enforcement (Powers and Responsibilities) Act* 2002.

[9]The issue of a right of independent appeal was prominent during parliamentary debate of Victoria's first banning bill in 2007, but a proposed amendment did not gain approval.

the more negative effects of discretionary police powers are outweighed by their potential benefits. However, such an assertion must be quantified, tested, and the subject of ongoing examination. The requirement for evidence-based policy development should form a core facet of *Charter Act* compliance in Victoria. The case for meaningful scrutiny is made even more compelling when core due process rights are curtailed under a presumption of advancing the 'greater good'.

References

Andrews, D. (2017). Powerful new laws to keep Victorians safe from terror. *Premier of Victoria Media Release, 21 September 2017*. Melbourne: State Government of Victoria. Available at: https://www.premier.vic.gov.au/wp-content/uploads/2017/09/170921-Powerful-New-Laws-To-Keep-Victorians-Safe-From-Terror.pdf.

Ashworth, A. (1996). Crime, community and creeping consequentialism. *Criminal Law Review*, 220–230.

Ashworth, A. (2004a). Social control and 'Anti Social Behaviour': The subversion of human rights? *Law Quarterly Review, 120*, 263–291.

Ashworth, A. (2004b). Criminal Justice Act 2003: Part 2: Criminal justice reform—principles, human rights and public protection. *Criminal Law Review*, 516–532.

Ashworth, A. (2006). Four threats to the presumption of innocence. *The International Journal of Evidence and Proof, 10*, 241–279.

Ashworth, A., & Redmayne, M. (2010). *The Criminal Process* (4th ed.). Oxford: Oxford University Press.

Ashworth, A., & Zedner, L. (2008). Defending the criminal law: Reflections on the changing character of crime, procedure and sanctions. *Criminal Law and Philosophy, 2*, 21–51.

Bronitt, S. (2008). Balancing security and liberty: Critical perspectives on terrorism law reform. In M. Gani & P. Mathew (Eds.), *Fresh perspectives on the 'War on Terror'* (pp. 65–84). Canberra: ANU.

Crawford, A. (2013). 'Sticks and carrots and sermons': Some thoughts on compliance and legitimacy in the regulation of youth anti-social behaviour. In A. Crawford & A. Hucklesby (Eds.), *Legitimacy and compliance in criminal justice* (pp. 181–214). Abingdon, Oxon: Routledge.

Curtis, A., Taylor, N., Guadagno, B., Farmer, C., & Miller, P. (2018). Community awareness of patron banning in Australia: A brief report. *Journal of Police and Criminal Psychology* [in press].

Damaska, M. R. (1975). Structures of authority and comparative criminal procedure. *Yale Law Journal, 84*, 480–544.

Dripps, D. A. (2011). The substance-procedure relationship in criminal Law. In R. A Duff & S. P Green (Eds.), *philosophical foundations of criminal law* (pp. 409–432). Oxford: Oxford University Press.

Dubber, M. D. (2002). Policing possession: The war on crime and the end of criminal law. *Journal of Criminal Law and Criminology, 91*(4), 829–996.

Dubber, M. D. (2005). The possession paradigm: The special part and the police power model of the criminal process. In R. A Duff & S. P Green (Eds.), *Defining crimes: Essays on the special part of the criminal law* (pp. 91–118). Oxford: Oxford University Press.

Dubber, M. D. (2006). Criminal law in comparative context. *Journal of Legal Education, 56*(3), 433–443.

Dubber, M. D. (2011). Regulatory and legal aspects of penality. In A. Sarat, L. Douglas, & M. M. Umphrey (Eds.), *Law as punishment, law as regulation* (pp. 19–49). Stanford, California: Stanford University Press.

Farmer, C., Curtis, A., & Miller, P. (2017). The steady proliferation of Australia's discretionary police-imposed banning powers: An unsubstantiated cycle of assertion and presumption. *Criminology & Criminal Justice* [published online 27/9/17].
Llewellyn, K. N. (1962). *Jurisprudence: Realism in theory and practice*. Chicago: Transaction Publishers.
Menendez P., Weatherburn D., & Kyrpi K., et al. (2015). Lockouts and last drinks: The impact of the January 2014 liquor licence reforms on assaults in NSW, Australia. *Crime and Justice Bulletin, 183* (April). Available at: http://www.bocsar.nsw.gov.au/Documents/CJB/CJB183.pdf.
Michaelsen, C. (2005). Antiterrorism legislation in Australia: A proportionate response to the terrorist threat? *Studies in Conflict and Terrorism, 28*(4), 321.
Michaelsen, C. (2006). Balancing civil liberties against national security? A critique of counter-terrorism Rhetoric. *UNSW Law Journal, 29*(2), 1–21.
Michaelsen, C. (2010). The proportionality principle, counter-terrorism laws and human rights: A German-Australian comparison. *City University of Hong Kong Law Review, 2*(1), 19–43.
Miller, P., Curtis, A., Palmer, D., et al. (2014). Changes in injury-related hospital emergency department presentations associated with the imposition of regulatory versus voluntary licensing conditions on licensed venues in two cities. *Drug and Alcohol Review, 33,* 314–322.
Miller, P., Curtis, A., Palmer, D., et al. (2016). Patron banning in the nightlife entertainment districts: A key informant perspective. *Journal of Studies on Alcohol & Drugs, 77*(4), 606–611.
Neocleous, M. (2007). Security, liberty and the myth of balance: Towards a critique of security politics. *Contemporary Political Theory, 6,* 131–149.
Packer, H. L. (1964). Two models of the criminal process. *University of Pennsylvania Law Review, 113*(1), 1–68.
Packer, H. L. (1968). *The limits of the criminal sanction*. Stanford, California: Stanford University Press.
Pue, W. W. (2008). Protecting constitutionalism in treacherous times: Why 'Rights' Don't matter. In M. Gani & P. Mathew (Eds.), *Fresh perspectives on the 'War on Terror'* (pp. 45–64). Canberra: ANU.
Roach, K. (1999). Criminology: Four models of the criminal process. *The Journal of Criminal Law and Criminology, 78*(2), 699–716.
Tonry, M. (2003). *Confronting crime: Crime control policy under new labour*. Abingdon, Oxon: Routledge.
Waldron, J. (2003). Security and liberty: The image of balance. *The Journal of Political Philosophy, 11*(2), 191–210.
Williams, G. (2006). The victorian charter of human rights and responsibilities: Origins and scope. *Melbourne University Law Review, 30,* 880–905.
Williams, G. (2007a). Victoria's new charter: Human rights and the community. *Just Policy, 43,* 6–10.
Williams, G. (2007b, February). Lessons from victoria's charter of human rights and responsibilities. *Law Society Journal*, 68–72.
Zedner, L. (2002). Dangers of dystopias in penal theory (extended review of David Garland, the culture of control: Crime and social order in contemporary society). *Oxford Journal of Legal Studies, 22*(2), 341–366.
Zedner, L. (2003). Too much security? *International Journal of the Sociology of Law, 31*(3), 155–184.
Zedner, L. (2005). Securing liberty in the face of terror; reflections from criminal justice. *Journal of Law and Society, 32*(4), 507–533.
Zedner, L. (2007a). Preventive justice or pre-punishment? the case of control orders. *Current Legal Problems, 60*(1), 174–2003.
Zedner, L. (2007b). Seeking security by eroding rights: The side-stepping of due process. In B. Goold & L. Lazarus (Eds.), *Security and human rights* (pp. 257–275). Oxford: Hart Publishing.
Zedner, L. (2007c). Pre-crime and post-criminology? *Theoretical Criminology, 11*(2), 261–281.
Zedner, L. (2014). Terrorising criminal law. *Criminal Law and Philosophy, 8,* 99–121.

FSC
www.fsc.org
MIX
Papier | Fördert gute Waldnutzung
FSC® C083411

Kolibri 360 GmbH
Ferdinand-Jühlke-Straße 7
99095 Erfurt, Deutschland
produktsicherheit@kolibri360.de